Training Guide

Microsoft Word

Second edition

Hari Andralojc, Pauline Walker
and Anne Lambden

Pitman

PITMAN PUBLISHING
128 Long Acre, London, WC2E 9AN

A Division of Longman Group UK Limited

© H Andralojc, A Lambden & P Walker 1987, 1990
First published in Great Britain 1987
Second edition published 1990
Reprinted 1991

British Library Cataloguing in Publication Data

Andralojc, Hari
  Microsoft Word.–(Word processor training
  guides).
  1. Microsoft Word (Computer program)
  I. Title II. Lambden, Ann III. Walker,
  Pauline IV. Series
652'.5'028553   Z52.5.M52
ISBN 0 273 03198 8

Acknowledgement

We should like to thank the staff of Hackney College for the use of the
computer equipment and facilities which were invaluable in the
production of this guide.

HA
AL
PW

Microsoft Word is a registered
trademark of Microsoft Corporation,
Reading, Berkshire.

Typeset by Tek Art Ltd, Croydon, Surrey
Printed and bound at The Bath Press, Avon

Contents

Introduction

This *Training Guide* is a practical introduction to the basic features of Microsoft Word ('Word'). It has been written for use on microcomputers with the **IBM PC** or **PS/2** style keyboards, including the **RM Nimbus** and the **Amstrad PC**.

Working the tasks   The same structure of instruction and exercise is maintained throughout the *Guide*. The instructions for performing a task are enclosed in a large box in the upper of the two pages. Words you are required to TYPE (eg Your Own Name) or keys to be tapped (eg Enter) are enclosed in boxes. It is assumed that you are using version 5.0 of the program and that the original settings on the program disk are in force.

Getting Started

If the following method of getting into Word does not apply exactly to the way your machine is set up, use your manual. If you are working on a network, check with your teacher/supervisor.

Starting Word   At step 2 below, choose the option that applies to your system:

1 Check the system prompt is onscreen (usually **A>** for a standalone machine or **C>** for a hard disk)
2 **360K floppy disks:**   insert the Program disk 1 into drive A and a formatted document disk into drive B

   Larger capacity disks: insert the Word program disk created by Setup into drive A, and a formatted disk for documents into drive B

   Hard disk system: TYPE cd directoryname , ie the name of the directory containing the Word program; and then tap Enter

3 TYPE word
4 Tap Enter . **360K system:** remove Program disk 1 and replace it with Program disk 2 when prompted

Setting up Word   After you have started Word and if you want to save files to a floppy disk in drive B:

1 Tap Esc ape, T ransfer, O ptions. At the **setup:** prompt
2 TYPE drivename: eg b: , for drive B
3 Tap Enter

Quitting Word
1 SAVE your work (*see* Task 4)
2 Tap Esc for Escape
3 Tap Q for Quit. If you have edited your work since last saving it the whole text becomes highlighted, and you will be prompted to **Enter Y to save changes to document, N to lose changes, or Esc to cancel** (the Quit command). Choose the one you want.

The Screen

WINDOW

Cursor (█)
containing
end mark (♦)

COMMAND AREA
Command Menu

COMMAND: Copy Delete Format Gallery Help Insert Jump Library
                    Options Print Quit Replace Search Transfer Undo Window
Edit document or press Esc to use menu

Message Line
Status Line

Pg1 Li1 Co1   { }   ?

Name of document

Microsoft Word

Scrap

Help mark
(mouse only)

Cursor position

Toggle keys status area

When Word is first loaded the screen looks like this. The screen is divided into two areas: a large **WINDOW**, covering most of the screen (it has been shortened above), with a smaller **COMMAND AREA** beneath it. The Line counter (**Li**) in the Status Line is optional. To set it up *see* the appendix (page 75).

WINDOW

This is where text is typed in and edited. The instructions in this *Training Guide* assume that the active cursor starts here. The keystroke in the Command Area which selects the text editing window is Esc for Escape. The text editing window is different from the **Window** command (not taught in this book).

The **cursor** is the point where text appears on the screen. It moves to the right as text is typed and may increase in size in the selection (highlighting) of text for editing or for executing commands. The diamond-shaped **end mark** (♦), initially contained within the cursor, marks the end of the document.

COMMAND AREA

When Word is first loaded, the cursor is located in the window. To execute most commands it is necessary to move it into the Command Area as the first step in selecting a command. While all the selection of text upon which commands may operate is done from within the window, only character and paragraph formatting commands, and 'toggle' commands (page 5), operate within it. All other text editing and file commands are made with an active cursor in the Command Area.

The **Command Menu** shows the main branches of the command tree available. The **Message Line** attempts to tell you what to do next, or what has gone wrong, or requests responses, at every stage of editing or using a command. The **Status Line** gives additional information. The **cursor position** indicators show the numbers of the page (**Pg**), the line (**Li**) and the column (**Co**) the cursor is in. It may also show the division number (**D**) eg **P1 D1 L1 C1**. The **Scrap** is a temporary store for deleted text, eg before being moved.

The **toggle keys status area** shows when the various keyboard locks are switched on (*see* page 5).

The **name of document** area shows the name of the document onscreen only after it has been saved, and the unbroken border until then.

Accessing the Command Area

Tap ⌷Esc⌷ for Escape. This highlights **Copy**, the first listed branch of the command tree. It is selected when Escape is tapped when the cursor is in the window.

Moving around the Command Area

Tap the first letter of the command (eg Tap ⌷T⌷ for Transfer). The active cursor enters that branch of the command tree. You will be faced with one or more **prompts**, words followed by a colon, eg **TRANSFER:**, which may not have responses already filled in. Some prompts have two or more **options**, one of which is always chosen, as indicated by the round brackets which enclose it, eg in **formatted: (Yes) No**, **Yes** is preselected. Preselected options, or values which are already filled in, are called defaults. They apply unless you deliberately choose a competing option or enter a different value. (The preset margin, **top: 1"**, is an example of a default value.)

> **To move between prompts and branches of the Command Tree:** use a combination of the arrowed direction keys (⌷←⌷, ⌷→⌷, ⌷↑⌷, ⌷↓⌷) **OR** tap the ⌷Tab⌷ key to move left to right and back to the beginning again

> **To select options within a prompt:** Tap the ⌷Spacebar⌷ to move left to right and back to the beginning again

Prompts and options are on a 'loop': eg tapping the ⌷→⌷ (⌷Right⌷) direction key at the last prompt takes the cursor back to the first.

Cancelling commands and returning to the window

When a command has been executed, the cursor is automatically returned to the text editing window.

A command may also be cancelled at nearly every stage:

Tap ⌷Esc⌷ for Escape to return the cursor to the window. (Exceptions: tap ⌷E⌷ for Exit to leave, HELP, GALLERY, PRINT PREVIEW and DOCUMENT-RETRIEVAL.) To start another command tap ⌷Esc⌷ again.

Undoing commands and editing

Even if a command has already been executed it can often be undone. Tap ⌷Esc⌷ for Escape, Tap ⌷U⌷ for Undo. This also applies to editing changes made in the window. See Task 11 for details.

Keyboard

The keyboard has the standard typewriter layout, but includes extra keys and symbols. Some standard symbols are in different places. If you are a touch-typist you will soon find out where. There are extra Shift keys and a number of keys with arrows on them (but there are no Shift-Lock keys to produce upper case letters and symbols). To avoid confusion between the different arrows the keys' names are used in the *Guide* instead of their symbols, except in the case of the four arrowed direction keys, where both are given. If you have an older keyboard, keys illustrated below with initial capitals may be all in capitals. The keys themselves may be different sizes.

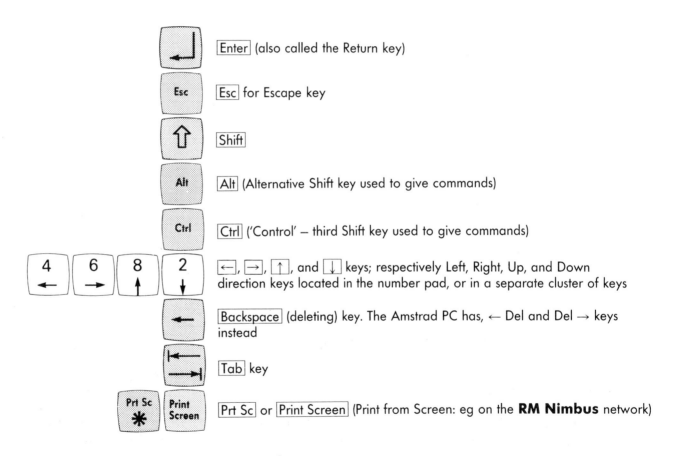

Enter (also called the Return key)

Esc for Escape key

Shift

Alt (Alternative Shift key used to give commands)

Ctrl ('Control' – third Shift key used to give commands)

←, →, ↑, and ↓ keys; respectively Left, Right, Up, and Down direction keys located in the number pad, or in a separate cluster of keys

Backspace (deleting) key. The Amstrad PC has, ← Del and Del → keys instead

Tab key

Prt Sc or Print Screen (Print from Screen: eg on the **RM Nimbus** network)

Toggle keys

Tapping a toggle key once turns a feature on. Tapping it again turns it off, rather like a light switch. Indeed, the **Number Lock**, **Caps Lock** and **Scroll Lock** keys will each have an indicator light if your keyboard is a recent one. There are nearly a dozen keystrokes which operate toggles. Some involve tapping one key, and the rest require one key to be held down while another is tapped. When the toggle keys are switched on a two-letter code appears in the Status Line (*see* the screen on page 2).

EX | Extend | highlight key, | F6 |, is on. *See* Task 10. Executing a command switches it off

NL | Number Lock | is on

SL | Scroll Lock | is on. *See* Task 19

CL | Caps Lock | is on. Typing in letters gives capitals; but typing in numbers from the number row still gives figures, not symbols. If | Caps Lock | is on and you hold down the | Shift | key, lower case letters are typed

OT | Overtype | key, | F5 |, is on

CS | Shift+F6 |, | Column Select | is on, *see* Task 23. Deleting a column also switches it off

LD | Ctrl+F5 |, | Line Draw | is on. You will be unable to type, except for drawing lines with the arrowed direction keys

If both **NL** and **LD**, or if both **EX** and **CS**, are switched on; only **NL** and **EX** respectively will show on the screen: both pairs of codes appear in the same places and **NL** and **EX** take priority if both are on.

In ordinary use the toggle keys should be kept switched off. The **Overtype**, **Number Lock**, and **Line Draw** functions are not needed for the whole book. It is very easy to switch on toggles by accident, causing unexpected problems when typing in text. The main culprits are the **Overtype (F5)**, **Caps Lock** and **Alt** keys (ie | Alt | plus another key, *see* Task 13). Should other two-letter codes appear, you will find it possible to continue typing. To clear the codes see the list in the **Appendix** on page 75.

Cancelling toggle keys

Repeat the keystroke.

Function keys

The function keys, or 'F' keys, are found in the pad of 10 keys at the left of the keyboard or the row of 12 keys at the top of the keyboard. Word is a powerful word processor and when the 'F' keys are used alone, or in combination with any of the shift keys (Ctrl, Shift, or Alt) extra commands are the result. Some of these are basic commands taught later; some are short cuts; others are advanced commands. All of them are potential sources of trouble for a beginner in Word. Therefore:

DO try not to tap the function keys by themselves, or in combination with the Control, Shift or Alt keys, until you know what they will do

DO watch the screen while you type or give commands so that if something goes wrong you can correct it as soon as possible (eg using Escape, Undo)

Presentation of keyboard commands

Many commands require the Ctrl, Shift or Alt keys to be held down while another key is tapped. The command is usually stated in full, eg 'hold down Alt and tap U for underlining'. Abbreviated it might appear as Alt+U. A sequence of keystrokes is occasionally shown, for example, as Escape, Transfer, Save. Tap the keys as indicated by the boxes rather than typing the letters: eg do not type the letters or the plus sign in Alt+U.

Help

Hold down Alt and tap H for Help, to get help information onscreen. For specific information about a command or a prompt or an option anywhere within that command:

1 Tap Esc for Escape (to select **Copy**)
2 Select the command or subcommand you want help with (*see* relevant Tasks and '**Moving around the Command Area**' on page 3 above)
3 Hold down Alt and tap H for Help

Cancelling help

Tap E for Exit. The active cursor is returned to the text editing window.

Task 1

Objective To type in text, watch wordwrap and make running corrections

Entering text Type in text as you would on a typewriter, but at the ends of lines do not tap Enter. Only tap Enter to start a new paragraph, after a heading, or to execute a command.

Running corrections If you made an error with your last keystroke, tap the Backspace key once to delete it. Type in the correct letter. Other ways of correcting errors are shown in later tasks. The Backspace key will not delete text if Overtype (F5) is switched on.

Memory jogger Check that the Status Line is clear of two-letter codes, which indicate that toggle keys are switched on. For example, if **CL** appears, the Caps Lock is on. Tap Caps Lock once to switch it off. If Overtype is on, tap F5 once to switch it off. (*See* 'Keyboard' on page 5 for a list of codes.)

Text creation
1 TYPE Your Own Name to identify your printout
2 Tap Enter 3 times to leave 2 clear lines after your name
3 TYPE in the text of Task 1. To start a new paragraph tap Enter twice. This leaves one clear line space
4 Correct any errors you notice at once, but, for this task only, leave any others you may make

Amendments Read through your work carefully. Note any errors you have made but do not correct them. SAVE your work under the filename: YourInitials1 (*see* Task 4) leaving no spaces or full stops between them; eg Jane Brown would type JB1. PRINT it (*see* Task 8). Circle any typing errors you made on the printout.

Task 1

You are now entering text onto the screen using a word processor.
Watch how the cursor moves across the screen as you type. Notice that
when you get to the end of each line, Word starts a new line for you
automatically. It moves the word you are typing to a new line when it
enters an invisible margin running down the right-hand side of the
screen. This feature is called wordwrap (or wraparound).

As well as saving you from having to break the flow of your typing by
tapping 'Enter' it also leaves the text on the screen in a flexible or
'unformatted' form. This means you can change its layout in many
different ways with great ease. For example, you could double the
width of the margins or reformat the text into several columns.

You may find it hard, at first, to remember not to tap the 'Enter' key
so frequently, but it is an important habit to get into for later on
when you will want to change the format of your documents.

Task 2

Objective To insert text and delete characters

Inserting text	Move the cursor to the character space where the text is to be inserted. Type in the missing character(s); or space(s) using the Spacebar.
Deleting characters	Move the cursor onto the character to be removed. Tap the Del for Delete key once. The character disappears from the window and reappears in the Scrap. (Tasks 10 and 11 look at the selection and deletion of blocks of text.)

Memory joggers **Overtype:** Word is set to insert text. Check that **OT** (for Overtype) does not appear in the Status Line. If it does appear there, tap the Overtype, F5, key once to switch it off.
If you delete a character by mistake, move the cursor to where it was lost and type it in again.

Text creation
1 TYPE Your Own Name
2 Tap Enter 3 times
3 TYPE in the text of Task 2

Amendments
1 First paragraph, third sentence: change 'a character' to 'characters' (delete 'a' and the space after it and type in an 's' at the end of 'character')
2 First paragraph, third sentence: change 'typing it in' to 'typing them in' (delete 'it' and insert 'them'). Leave one character space between 'them' and 'in'
3 Second paragraph, first sentence: change 'a key' to 'the keys' (delete 'a' and insert 'the'; add an 's' at the end of 'key')
4 Second paragraph, first sentence: change 'hold it down' to 'hold them down' (delete 'it' and insert 'them')
5 Third paragraph, first sentence: change 'The best keyboard has' to 'Some keyboards have' (delete 'The best' and insert 'Some', add an 's' at the end of 'keyboard', delete the 's' at the end of 'has' and insert 've' in its place)

Read through your work carefully and correct any errors you find. SAVE it under the filename YourInitials2 (*see* Task 4) and PRINT it (*see* Task 8).

Task 2

When you delete using Word, no gap is left where the wrong character(s) had been. The text 'closes up' as if the error had never been made. When you insert a character you don't have to make a space before typing it in. If inserting pushes a word into the invisible right-hand margin, the wordwrap feature automatically moves it to the next line.

As well as getting used to tapping 'Enter' less often, you should try to get a feel for how hard to tap a key and how long to hold it down. Unless you have to hold down one key (ie Shift, Ctrl or Alt) while you tap another, the general rule is to tap the keys lightly, as you would on an electronic typewriter.

The best keyboard has a 'click-touch'. You feel a soft click through your fingers before you have pressed a key as far as it will go. The click means the word processor has typed that character onto the screen. It helps you to build up speed and keeps your fingers from getting so tired, as well as prolonging the life of the keyboard.

Most of the keys on a word processor's keyboard are 'repeater' keys. If you press a key and hold it down rather than just tapping it, you will type the same character again and again; or, if you are deleting text, you may delete more than you meant to - so keep your touch light.

Task 3

Objective To join and split paragraphs

Joining paragraphs	Move the cursor onto the very first letter of the paragraph which is to be joined to the end of the paragraph above it. Tap Backspace until they join (ie twice, if one line separates the paragraphs). Insert spaces as necessary.
Splitting paragraphs	Move the cursor onto the first letter of the word which is to become the first letter of the new paragraph. Tap Enter twice. This leaves one clear line space between the paragraphs.
Inserting blank line spaces	1 Move the cursor to a blank line or on to the first character of the text to follow the blank lines 2 Tap Enter once for each additional line space required (there are 6 per inch)

Memory jogger Check that the Status Line contains no two-letter codes (*see* page 5) so that eg Caps Lock (**CL**) and Overtype (**OT**) are both switched off.

Text creation
1 TYPE Your Own Name
2 Tap Enter 3 times
3 TYPE in the text of Task 3. Use the Caps Lock key to type 'PROOFREADING'. Immediately afterwards, tap Caps Lock again to switch it off

Amendments
1 Make 'PROOFREADING' a heading by starting a new paragraph at the 'T' of 'Throw away'
2 Start a new paragraph at 'Proofreading means reading'
3 Start a new paragraph at 'As a double-check'
4 Join the last 3 paragraphs together. Make sure there are 2 character spaces between the sentences
5 In the newly created last paragraph start a new paragraph at the 'M' of 'Mistakes do not'

Read through your work carefully and correct any errors you find. SAVE it under the filename YourInitials3 (*see* Task 4) and PRINT it (*see* Task 8).

Task 3

PROOFREADING Throw away your correcting fluid! Using a word
processor, all corrections are carried out on the screen before a
document is printed. Proofreading means reading each word of your work
carefully and also making sure the layout is right. When you have
typed in your work, move the cursor back to the very beginning and use
it to guide your eyes by moving it down the screen at the left-hand
margin as you check each line. As a double-check you should read
through a document after it has been printed, especially if it is going
to be sent to an important customer.

Make sure your paragraphs have at least one clear line space between
them and that there are consistently 1, 2 or 3 character spaces after a
full stop, a question mark and an exclamation mark.

There should be one space after a comma, a semi-colon and a colon
within the body of your work and one space between each word.

There should also be at least one clear line space above and below a
shoulder heading. Mistakes do not disappear of their own accord, and
the text on the screen will be saved and printed exactly as it appears.
Make sure it is error-free by always proofreading your work.

Task 4

Objective   To save work, clear the screen and abandon work

Saving work
1 Tap ⬜Esc for Escape
2 Tap ⬜T for Transfer
3 Tap ⬜S for Save. The cursor now lies next to the prompt **TRANSFER SAVE filename:** and the Message Line requests you to **Enter filename**
4 TYPE in a ⬜filename using the rules of Task 4 below. Check the **format** prompt selects (**Word**)
5 If it doesn't, tap the ⬜↓, ⬜Down, key once and then tap the ⬜Spacebar until it does
6 Tap ⬜Enter. In the Message Line: **Saving . . . JB4** tells you that Word is saving your file
7 When saving a file for the first time a **SUMMARY INFORMATION** menu may be displayed. Ignore it
8 Tap ⬜Esc for Escape to finish saving. (Tapping ⬜Enter will not always work.)

If the message: **File already exists. Enter Y to replace or Esc to cancel** appears, the filename you have chosen belongs to another file, which you risk overwriting. Tap ⬜N for No and use a different filename. A file you overwrite is lost. If the message **Not a valid filename** appears, your filename does not obey the rules. Change it until it does. The filename is displayed in the lower border of the window.

Clearing the screen
When a document has been saved it should be cleared from the screen before typing in a new document and not merely deleted (which introduces the danger of unknowingly overwriting the file just saved).

1 Tap ⬜Esc for Escape
2 Tap ⬜T for Transfer
3 Tap ⬜C for Clear
4 Tap ⬜W for Window. If you have just saved the document, the screen will clear. If you have edited the document since last saving it, the prompt: **Enter Y to save changes to document, N to lose changes, or Esc to cancel** appears in the Message Line
5 Tap ⬜Y for Yes, to save it and clear the screen

To abandon work   Do not save it. Clear the screen as above and tap ⬜N to lose changes.

Text creation
1 TYPE ⬜Your Own Name
2 Tap ⬜Enter 3 times
3 TYPE in the text of Task 4. Use the ⬜Caps Lock key to type in the heading. Remember to switch it off
4 At the ends of short lines tap ⬜Enter

Amendments
1 Proofread and correct your work. SAVE it under the filename ⬜YourInitials4. PRINT it (*see* Task 8)
2 Clear the screen.

Task 4

RULES FOR FILENAMES

Text saved by a word processor is put into a file which is kept
separate from other documents. A filename is the name given to such
text to identify it to you and to Word. When you save a document, Word
asks you to enter a filename. This filename should obey the following
rules. If it doesn't obey the first two rules, Word will not save it
until it does:

1 A filename can be up to 8 characters long;
2 A filename may not contain spaces and most punctuation marks,
except hyphens, round brackets and a few others;
3 A filename may be typed in using either lower or upper case letters;
4 Every file on the same disk must have a different filename;
5 Every file, wherever it is stored, should have a different filename.

If you know you will want to keep a document while you are typing it,
save it when you pause for thought, and always when you leave your
workstation. Until your work is saved it could be lost by accident.

Task 5

<table>
<tr><td>Objective</td><td colspan="2">To load (retrieve) files and rename them</td></tr>
</table>

Objective   To load (retrieve) files and rename them

Loading files

1 If there is a document onscreen you want to keep, SAVE it (*see* Task 4)
2 Tap Esc for Escape
3 Tap T for Transfer
4 Tap L for Load. The prompt **TRANSFER LOAD filename:** appears in the Command Area
5 TYPE in the filename of the text to be loaded. It is not necessary to type '.doc' to load a file which uses this extension. The filename extension must be typed to load a file with any other extension
6 Tap Enter

If the message: **Enter Y to save changes to document, N to lose changes, or Esc to cancel** appears, you have edited a file and not yet saved it again. Tap Y for Yes to save it again. If the message **File does not exist. Enter Y to create or Esc to cancel** appears, the filename has not been used.

Renaming files

1 Load the file to be renamed
2 Tap Esc for Escape
3 Tap T for Transfer
4 Tap R for Rename. The prompt **TRANSFER RENAME filename:** appears in the Command Area with the old filename which will be preceded by other 'technical' details, eg **C: \ WORD \ or B: **
5 TYPE in the new filename **on top of the old one** regardless of any other details displayed
6 Tap Enter. If the message **Cannot rename file** appears, you have chosen a filename which is already in use. Follow steps 2 to 5 again, but using a different filename

Copying files   To copy a file, save it using a new filename. Renaming it merely renames the original version.

Memory jogger   Caps Lock will only type letters in upper case. For punctuation and symbols, use the Shift key.

Text creation

1 TYPE Your Own Name
2 Tap Enter 3 times
3 TYPE in the text of Task 5

Amendments

1 Proofread your work and correct it if necessary
2 SAVE it under the filename Task5YourInitials (*see* Task 4). The full filename: Task5YourInitials.doc, appears in the lower border of the window
3 Rename it YourInitials5 and clear the screen (*see* Task 4)
4 Load the file YourInitials5 and PRINT a copy (*see* Task 8).

Task 5

FILENAME EXTENSIONS

The full stop and the three letters which Word has added to your
document filenames are called a filename extension.

When you name a document of your own, you can add your own filename
extension to help you distinguish it from other types of files. For
example, you could use: .ltr, for standard letters; .dat, for datafiles
of names and addresses and .doc for general documents only.

You should work out what your needs are and compile a list of suitable
filename extensions. It helps if a filename extension reminds you of
the type of file it represents; as '.dat' could do because it is very
nearly 'data'.

BACK-UP FILES

A back-up is a spare copy of a file. When you type in a document,
saving it from time to time, Word does not destroy the very last
version that you saved but renames it as a back-up copy. This has the
same filename as the current version but with a different filename
extension; .BAK for back-up copy. For example, the back-up of the file
HOLIDAYS.DOC would have the filename HOLIDAYS.BAK. This means that if
you decide you don't like the changes in the new version (HOLIDAYS.DOC)
you can load the old version (HOLIDAYS.BAK) and work from that instead.
However, only the last version is saved; any earlier versions are lost.
In other words, even if you have saved your document more than once,
you will have two versions altogether, but no more; unless you save
them under different filenames.

Task 6

Objective

To load files (continued), and to view the directory of files

Loading files (second method)

If you are unsure of the name of a '.DOC' file to be loaded:

1 Load as before. Tap ⎡Esc⎤ape, ⎡T⎤ransfer, ⎡L⎤oad. In response to the prompt **TRANSFER LOAD filename:**
2 Tap ⎡F1⎤. This displays the list of '.DOC' files in the current directory
3 Select the file to be loaded using the direction keys. If the screen looks full of files use the direction keys to view any files that may be offscreen. (Move the cursor to the bottom of the screen and tap the ⎡↓⎤, ⎡Down⎤, direction key to see if there are any more lower down; not onscreen.)
4 Tap ⎡Enter⎤ (or tap ⎡Esc⎤ for Escape instead, to resume editing without loading a file)

Viewing the directory

To view files with a different extension, eg .LTR, .BAK, .DAT:

1 Tap ⎡Esc⎤ for Escape
2 Tap ⎡T⎤ for Transfer
3 Tap ⎡L⎤ for Load
4 TYPE ⎡*.ltr⎤, ⎡*.bak⎤, ⎡*.dat⎤ for whichever group of files is required
5 Tap ⎡F1⎤. The list of all the files in the directory with the extension chosen will be screened

Memory jogger

To abort a command tap ⎡Esc⎤ for Escape to re-enter the window.

Text creation

1 TYPE ⎡Your Own Name⎤
2 Tap ⎡Enter⎤ 3 times
3 TYPE in the text of Task 6

Amendments

1 Proofread and correct your work and SAVE it under the filename ⎡YourInitials6⎤ (*see* Task 4)
2 PRINT a copy (*see* Task 8)
3 Use the information in the text of Task 6 (and above) to prepare your own manual log of files
4 Make entries in your manual log for the files you have created up to now. Keep your manual log for use with the tasks which follow
5 View any .BAK files you have created. Write a 'B' beside the appropriate entries in your manual log if those files have a back-up copy.

Task 6

FILE MANAGEMENT

It is very easy to get into a muddle with your files, especially when you are busy or need to use several disks to store them. If you have to use files created by someone else, finding out which file you want to retrieve can be like looking for a needle in a haystack, particularly if that person is out of the office.

One way to overcome this problem is to keep a neat manual log of all the files you have access to in a separate notebook which lists the following information:

date file created, author, filename, disk number, date and time revised, brief description.

You should make an entry in the manual log at the time a file is created or updated, because you will forget to do it later.

Some word processors have a detailed directory attached to the files created. In this case the details can be entered here whenever a file is amended and a printout obtained at will.

Task 7

Objective	To delete files

Before deleting a file make sure that it is no longer required. If there is any doubt do not delete it. The file could be copied to another disk if space is a problem on the current working disk. File deletion (using **TRANSFER DELETE**) cannot be undone. You cannot delete the file which is on the screen.

Deleting files

1 Tap Esc for Escape
2 Tap T for Transfer
3 Tap D for Delete. At the prompt **TRANSFER DELETE filename:**
4 TYPE the complete filename of the file to be deleted, ie including its filename extension. **Check** that you have typed **exactly** the filename you wanted. Otherwise you may delete the wrong file
5 Tap Enter. In response to the message **Enter Y to confirm deletion of file**
6 Tap Y for Yes

If the above method fails to delete the file:

1 Clear the screen by tapping Esc ape, T ransfer, C lear, W indow, (see Task 4)
2 Proceed as in '**Deleting files**' above

Memory jogger

When the Message Line says **Enter filename or press F1 to select from list**, tap F1 to see the list.

Text creation

1 TYPE Your Own Name
2 Tap Enter 3 times
3 TYPE in the text of Task 7

Amendments

1 Proofread your work and correct it if necessary
2 SAVE it using the filename Task7YourInitials (see Task 4) and record its details in your manual log
3 PRINT a copy (see Task 8)
4 SAVE it again using the filename YourInitials7. View the directory to verify that the file has been saved under both filenames (see Task 6)
5 Try to delete the file YourInitials7.doc; which should be onscreen. The attempt will fail. Note the message: **Cannot delete file**. This shows you cannot delete the task onscreen
6 Delete the file Task7YourInitials.doc. If you do not type in the full filename, then after tapping Y for Yes the message: **File or directory does not exist** will be displayed
7 Check the directory again to verify that the file Task7YourInitials.doc has now been deleted.

Task 7

If your system uses a hard disk it is reasonably safe from damage in
its casing. Floppy disks, however, are loose and need to be numbered
and kept in good order. They should be kept in a rigid container made
for the purpose and stored in a secure place.

The only disks you should need to use regularly are working copies of
master disks. Back-up copies of working disks should be made
frequently so that if a disk is accidentally damaged, not too much work
is lost.

From time to time, you should delete unwanted entries from your manual
log of files and the unwanted files themselves from working disks. In
a business, copies of letters printed and sent might be the first to
go: you would have taken 'hard' copies of them already if needed for
records.

In a hospital or a bank, where records have to be kept for a long time,
the files would not be deleted routinely, but stored in archives until
the expiry of the prescribed storage period.

Task 8

Objective To print work

Printing active document	Ensure your printer is switched on and ready to print. (We assume the correct printer driver has been loaded.)

1 Tap `Esc` for Escape
2 Tap `P` for Print
3 Tap `P` for Printer. The message **Printing page 1 of . . . YOURINITIALS8.DOC** appears in the Message Line. (The '8' refers to Task 8.)
4 Wait for printing to end as indicated by the reappearance of the Command Menu, before typing any more commands. If you are working on the **RM Nimbus** network WAIT for the Command Menu to reappear and then:
5 Hold down `Ctrl` and `Alt` together and tap `Prt Sc` (or `Print Screen`) for Print from Screen

Cancelling printing

1 Tap `Esc` for Escape, as quickly as possible. In response to the prompt: **Enter Y to continue or Esc to cancel**
2 Tap `Y` for Yes to resume printing, or `Esc` for Escape to halt the print. If your document is short you will not be able to stop it being printed unless you tap `Esc` for Escape very quickly

(Note. Your first prints may involve some trial and error while you learn how to set up the printer.)

Memory Jogger **Undo:** to reverse a command or piece of editing: tap `Esc` for Escape, then `U` for Undo as soon as you notice something has gone wrong. You may be too late. If you do not like the effect of undoing, you can even 'undo' the undoing by repeating the command. You cannot undo printing.

Text creation

1 TYPE `Your Own Name`
2 Tap `Enter` 3 times
3 TYPE in the text of Task 8

Amendments

1 Proofread your work. Correct any mistakes you find while the Task is still onscreen
2 SAVE it using the filename `YourInitials8` (*see* Task 4). Record its details in your manual log of files
3 PRINT it
4 Clear the screen (*see* Task 4).

Task 8

PRINTERS

The end product of your work as a word processor operator is the printout of the letter or document you have typed. This is called 'hard' copy as opposed to the intangible 'soft' copy on your screen. The quality of the printout required by you or your company dictates the type of printer to use.

A letter-quality printer uses a 'daisy-wheel' printing element to produce documents which look as though they have been typed on an electronic typewriter. It takes about a minute to print a full A4 page.

For draft work the dot matrix printer is popular. It is cheaper and faster than a daisy-wheel printer. The characters are formed from tiny dots of ink poked on to the paper.

Some printers combine both daisy-wheel and dot matrix printing elements in one machine.

The future of high-quality printing in businesses belongs to laser printers. They print several times faster than dot matrix printers. They are quiet and clean, fit on a desk top and will soon match the quality of print produced by typesetting. As well as typed text, they can produce large headings and graphics.

Task 9

Objective   To operate fast cursor movements

Cursor movement

Cursor movement (or direction) keys are located in the number pad at the right of the keyboard (or in a cluster of direction keys to the left of the number pad) and in the function key pad (*see* page 6).

(Notes. Shift+F7 means hold down Shift and tap F7 once. Spaces and punctuation marks may be treated by Word as either words or sentences or paragraphs when moving the cursor.)

F7 moves the cursor to the left word by word   Shift+F7 moves it back sentence by sentence
F8 moves the cursor to the right word by word   Shift+F8 moves it forwards sentence by sentence
F9 moves the cursor up paragraph by paragraph   F10 moves it down paragraph by paragraph

Home moves the cursor to the start of the line the cursor is in
End moves the cursor to the end of the line the cursor is in
Pg Up moves the cursor up one screenful of text until the first line of the document can be seen
Pg Dn moves the cursor down one screenful of text, or onto the last line or end mark (♦) if there is less than one screen's depth before the end of the document. (Pg Up = Page Up, Pg Dn = Page Down.)

Ctrl+←, Ctrl+→, move the cursor respectively left and right to the first character of a word
Ctrl+Home   moves the cursor up to the top left-hand corner of the screen
Ctrl+End   moves the cursor down to the bottom left-hand corner of the screen
Ctrl+Pg Up   moves the cursor to the start of the document
Ctrl+Pg Dn   moves the cursor to the end mark, (♦), the extreme end of the document

Memory joggers

The arrowed direction keys (←, →, ↑, ↓, respectively Left, Right, Up and Down) move the cursor respectively left or right one character space, up or down one line. In the Command Area they move the cursor between prompts and between branches of the Command tree.
Number Lock: must be switched off if cursor movement keys on the number pad are to be used (page 5).

Text creation

1   TYPE Your Own Name
2   Tap Enter 3 times
3   TYPE in the text of Task 9

Amendments

1   Proofread your work and correct any mistakes you find
2   SAVE it using the filename YourInitials9 (*see* Task 4) and record its details in your manual log
3   Practise using all the fast cursor movement keystrokes
4   PRINT a copy (*see* Task 8).

Task 9

MOVING AROUND DOCUMENTS

There is quite a lot of skill in moving quickly around the documents
you create. Some people tend to use the arrowed direction keys too
much and neglect the more powerful methods available, especially if
they have not been trained to use a word processor. Working in a busy
office, people have little time to learn the best way and may just 'get
by', using the first cursor movements they learned. Sometimes it is
difficult to do more because of an instruction manual which is hard to
understand.

Just as it was important to get used to pressing 'Enter' less
frequently, so it is also important to get into the habit of moving
around a document quickly and accurately.

The simple idea to follow is that the quickest way is the best way.
The 'quickest way' is the way which takes the fewest keystrokes. So
think about how you are moving around your documents and try to put the
wide range of cursor movements to their best use.

While the exercises in this book are quite small and it is possible to
get around using the simple cursor movements alone, you should practise
using the faster ones because in longer documents you will need to be
able to use all the short cuts you can.

Task 10

Objective To select text for reformatting

Selection of text

Text to be moved, copied, deleted or otherwise reformatted must usually be selected (or highlighted) using the cursor. The same keys are used to highlight text as to move around it, and the two functions should be used in combination.

F7	selects the 'word' the cursor is in	Shift+F7	selects the sentence the cursor is in
F8	selects the 'word' the cursor is in	Shift+F8	selects the sentence the cursor is in
F9	selects the paragraph the cursor is in	Shift+F9	selects the line the cursor is in
F10	selects the paragraph the cursor is in	Shift+F10	selects the whole document

Extending the selection

1 Move the cursor to one end of the block of text to be selected
2 Tap F6 (the Extend selection key) to anchor the cursor ('**EX**' appears in the Status Line)
3 To extend the highlighting of text use the keystrokes listed above, listed in Task 9 and the arrowed direction keys (Note. Shift+direction key(s) has a similar effect.)

Cancelling selection

Tap a cursor movement (direction) key. The cursor will be returned to its original size and moved to a point just outside where the highlight had been depending on the key tapped. To cancel the anchoring of the cursor by the Extend key tap F6 once. '**EX**' disappears from the Status Line.

Memory jogger

The F7, F8, Shift+F7, Shift+F8, F9 and F10 keystrokes can also be used to move the cursor quickly (*see* Task 9). Use the keys for both highlighting text and for moving.

Text creation

1 TYPE Your Own Name
2 Tap Enter 3 times
3 TYPE in the text of Task 10

Amendments

1 Proofread and correct your work. SAVE it using the filename YourInitials10 and PRINT a copy
2 Practise selecting different blocks of text using all the keystrokes above. Here are some suggestions:
3 Select the first word of the first sentence. Count the number of words in this sentence using the F8 key. (Ignore punctuation marks and spaces between words in your count.) Check your result by counting backwards using the F7 key
4 Select the first sentence of the second paragraph. Extend the selection to include the second sentence
5 Select the third paragraph. Tap the ↓, Down, key to cancel the selection
6 Select the second and third lines, not sentences, of the last paragraph. Cancel the selection
7 Select the whole document. Tap the ↑, Up, direction key to move to the start of the selection.

Task 10

FIT FOR WORK?

Good health is a preoccupation of our age and much has been written on
the subject. For those who work within the confines of an office,
reducing the fatigue of a desk job is vital for one's general well-
being.

Your brain needs oxygen and that means you should breathe plenty of
fresh air. Can you open the windows in your office? Do you go out
at lunch-time?

If you spend most of your working day sitting down, then you are urged
to take up some form of exercise. Evening classes for badminton or
keep-fit are good fun and can lead to further social events. Walking
and swimming are activities which can be as gentle or as vigorous as
you care to make them. Many people have recently discovered the
health club or gymnasium where machines are used to work and tone
different parts of the body.

Do you always take the lift to the next floor or to the one above?
Try using the stairs for a change. If you make it a habit, you'll soon
find you are breathing evenly when you arrive and won't feel the need
to lie down in a darkened room to recover from your exertions!

Task 11

Objective	To delete blocks of text and undo editing changes

Text deletion	1 Select the text to be deleted (*see* Task 10) 2 Tap the Del for Delete key once only. The text selected disappears from the window into the Scrap. If you realise your deletion was a mistake before moving the cursor elsewhere, tap Ins for Insert to replace the text deleted. If you realise it later you will have to undo the edit
Undoing	If an editing change or the execution of a command was a mistake, you can frequently 'undo' the error if you notice it in time; ie (generally) before you do any more editing, or give any more commands. 1 Tap Esc for Escape 2 Tap U for Undo. If your edit was a deletion, this command inserts the text deleted from the Scrap into its original place in the document before deletion. If undoing is unsuccessful, or if you preferred your document the way it was before undoing, Undo a second time. This restores the document to the way it was before the first Undo command
Commands you cannot undo	Print, Options, Quit, and Transfer commands, except Transfer Merge (Task 31) cannot be undone. They can only be cancelled before execution.
Special deletion	Select the text to be deleted, then hold down Shift and tap Del for Delete. The Shift+Del command bypasses the Scrap. Only use it to protect the contents of the Scrap while erasing. It can be undone.

Memory jogger	**Keyboard:** tap the Del for Delete key smartly but with caution. Re-read about deletion on page 10.
Text creation	1 TYPE Your Own Name 2 Tap Enter 3 times 3 TYPE in the text of Task 11. Watch the Scrap while you carry out the amendments
Amendments	1 Proofread, correct, SAVE and log your work (filename: YourInitials11, *see* Task 4). PRINT it (Task 8) 2 First paragraph: delete the last sentence 3 Delete the second paragraph and leave one line space between the remaining paragraphs 4 Paragraph starting 'In Word...'. Delete the word 'highlighted' 5 Same paragraph: select and delete the phrase 'using the Del for Delete key'. **Do not** move the cursor 6 Tap Ins for Insert to replace the phrase 7 Delete the same phrase again and tap Ctrl+End to move to the bottom of the window. Undo the deletion.

Task 11

A computer has several different kinds of memory. One of these is the
memory into which programs are read when you first load the system disk
or a program disk. It is called RAM and is the amount of memory people
talk about when they say 'it's a 640K computer'.

The computer 'forgets' whatever is stored in RAM when it is switched
off; which is why it is so important to save to disk any files you have
created beforehand.

A word processing program also has different types of memory. Their
purpose is to let you delete text safely or to move it around one
document or between several.

In Word the simplest memory is the 'scrap' - so called because it
usually contains scraps of text. It is the pair of braces (curly
brackets) in the Status Line. Whenever you delete highlighted text
using the Del for Delete key, it disappears from the text editing
window into the scrap. It is on its way out, but it has not gone for
good - yet.

The Undo command gives you a second chance when you delete a block of
text in error by allowing you to replace it in the document exactly
where it came from. But do not wait before putting it back. The scrap
can only hold one item, the last block deleted, so put it back where it
belongs before you delete anything else.

Task 12

Objective To move and copy blocks of text

Moving text
1 Highlight the text to be moved (*see* Task 10)
2 Tap Esc for Escape
3 Tap D for Delete in the Command Menu (**not** Del for Delete on the keyboard, **and not** Transfer Delete in the Command Area!)
4 Tap Enter. The text has been deleted to the Scrap
5 Move the cursor to the point where the text is to be inserted
6 Tap Ins for Insert

Copying text
1 Highlight the text to be copied (*see* Task 10)
2 Tap Esc for Escape
3 Tap C for Copy
4 Follow steps 4–6 above. In step 4 the text will be copied to the Scrap

Memory joggers If you select the wrong block of text, tap one of the direction keys to clear the selection and start again.
If your selection involved tapping the Extend selection key F6, tap F6 again to remove the anchor from the cursor before starting again.
Paragraphs should have, consistently, at least one clear line space between them.

Text creation
1 TYPE Your Own Name
2 Tap Enter 3 times
3 TYPE in the text of Task 12

Amendments
1 Move the fifth paragraph ('TABLES:... leg room?') so that it becomes the second one
2 Adjust the line spacing so that there is a clear line space between the paragraphs
3 Copy the last sentence of the first paragraph and insert it as a separate paragraph at the end of the task, one clear line space below the paragraph starting 'NOISE...'
4 Delete the last sentence of the first paragraph

Proofread your work and correct any mistakes you find. SAVE it using the filename YourInitials12 (*see* Task 4) and record its details in your manual log of files (Task 6). PRINT it (*see* Task 8).

Task 12

HEALTH AND SAFETY IN THE OFFICE

You might be fit for work, but is your office? Offices can be
refreshing, stimulating places to work, or they can add greatly to the
tiredness you will feel at the end of a working day. Colleagues apart,
the surroundings are very important. Here are a few items for a
checklist. Try scoring '2' for good, '1' for average and '0' for poor
and see how well your office does.

LIGHTING: is there much glare on the screen of the machine you will be
working at due to the room lighting or the light from the windows?

SCREEN: are the characters crisp and easy to read, or are they too
small, or blurred? Does the screen flicker?

SEATING: are there proper operators' chairs? Can they be adjusted for
height; do they have firm back supports?

TABLES: is your terminal on a typist's table or a clerk's? Does it
give you enough leg room?

CABLING: do the many cables from the computers and printers trail all
over the place, or are they safely hidden inside trunking?

NOISE: how quiet is the printer? Are daisy-wheel printers shielded
under acoustic hoods, or left to clatter away on desks every time
someone prints a document?

Task 13

Objective	To reformat characters

Character reformatting . . .
A suitable monitor and a printer appropriately set up are needed to produce all the character formats. It is easier to reformat text after typing it in (rather than before) until you have had some practice.

. . . After typing
1 Highlight the text to be reformatted (*see* Task 10)
2 Hold down Alt and tap the appropriate key(s) as in step 1 of '. . . **Before typing**' below
3 Tap a cursor key to reveal the change(s). Only the highlighted (selected) text is reformatted

. . . Before typing
1 Hold down Alt and tap B for Boldface   Hold down Alt and tap K for small capitals
Hold down Alt and tap I for Italics   Hold down Alt and tap = for superscript
Hold down Alt and tap U for Underlining   Hold down Alt and tap - (hyphen) for subscript
Hold down Alt and tap S for Strikethrough   Hold down Alt and tap E for hidden text*
Hold down Alt and tap D for Double underlining   *not taught in this book

2 TYPE in the text to have the new format
3 Hold down Alt and tap the Spacebar. Characters typed now will have the ordinary format

Cancelling character reformatting
1 Select the text to be returned to the default character format
2 Hold down Alt and tap the Spacebar
3 Tap a cursor key to reveal the change(s)

Memory joggers
Default. The default is the setting or choice you get unless you deliberately choose something else. If you accidentally reformat characters wrongly, undo the reformatting straight away.

Text creation
1 TYPE Your Own Name
2 Tap Enter 3 times
3 TYPE in the text of Task 13

Amendments
1 Give the task a heading 'HEADING AND PARAGRAPH STYLES'. Embolden and underline it
2 First paragraph. Reformat the word 'consistency' in boldface type and italics
3 First paragraph. Strike through the second, third and fourth sentences
4 Fourth paragraph. Reformat the phrase 'complimentary close' in boldface type and italics

Proofread, correct, SAVE and log your work (filename: YourInitials13, *see* Task4). PRINT it (*see* Task 8).

Task 13

The professional presentation of a document depends on consistency of style throughout its length. At work you are quite likely to have to follow a house style. At home you are free to choose your own. Whatever style you choose it should be followed consistently. If you are unsure which style to use you may find the following conventions helpful.

The simplest style is to block all headings and text at the left-hand margin. Any text inset from the margin should also be blocked.

If you block paragraphs at the left-hand margin, then headings may be either blocked or centred. The same applies to hanging paragraphs. If centring is to be used for main headings, then sub-headings may be either centred or blocked.

The complimentary close (Yours sincerely, etc) should always be blocked in a letter with blocked paragraphs. It is unusual to use hanging paragraphs in letters.

If you indent paragraphs, all headings should be centred. In a letter, the complimentary close starts at the centre of the page.

Task 14

Objective   To reformat paragraphs

Paragraph reformatting . . .	This means changing the appearance and/or position of paragraphs from their default settings. The novice to word processing might find it easier to reformat text after typing it in than before. (Insetting and indenting paragraphs are dealt with in Tasks 24 to 26.)
. . . After typing	1 Select (highlight) the paragraph(s) to be reformatted (*see* Task 10) 2 Hold down Alt and tap the appropriate key(s) as in '**. . . Before typing**' below 3 Tap any direction key to remove the highlighting from the text
. . . Before typing	1 Hold down Alt and tap C for Centring Hold down Alt and tap L for Left flush Hold down Alt and tap J for Justification Hold down Alt and tap R for Right flush Hold down Alt and tap 2 for Double line spacing Hold down Alt and tap O for Open paragraph spacing (to insert a blank line in front of a paragraph) 2 TYPE in the text to have the new format (tapping Enter at least twice at the ends of paragraphs) 3 Tap Enter at the end of the last paragraph to have the new format 4 Hold down Alt and tap P for Plain paragraph format for the paragraphs to follow
Cancelling paragraph reformatting	1 Select the paragraph(s) displayed in a new format which are to be returned to the original format 2 Hold down Alt and tap P for Plain paragraph format 3 Tap any direction key to remove the highlighting from the text

Memory joggers   Any line after which you have pressed Enter is regarded by Word as being a paragraph.
Tap a direction key to cancel highlighting. Tap Esc for Escape, U for Undo to cancel a command.

Text creation
1 TYPE Your Own Name
2 Tap Enter 3 times
3 TYPE in the text of Task 14

Amendments
1 Select the lines, from 'FOR SALE' to 'Tel: 010 7834-0287' (use F6 and the ↓ , Down , key) and centre them
2 Double the double line spacing of the first four lines using Alt+2

Proofread, correct, SAVE and log your work (filename: YourInitials14 , *see* Task 4). PRINT it (*see* Task 8).

Task 14

F O R   S A L E

Rolls Royce Silver Ghost

£20,000 (Quick Sale)

Tel: 010 7834-0287

Leaving the country in a hurry, I am regrettably forced to part with
this family treasure at a fraction of its true value. Condition
immaculate as only used indoors.

Task 15

Objective
To combine character and paragraph reformatting

Combining formats
Character reformatting can be combined with paragraph reformatting to give more elaborate effects. It is easier to combine formats after typing in text than before.

. . . After typing
1. Highlight the text to be reformatted (*see* Task 10)
2. Hold down Alt and tap, one after the other, the keys which will give the character and/or paragraph formats you want (*see* Tasks 13, 14 and 24 to 26)

. . . Before typing
Hold down Alt and tap, one after the other, the keys which will give the formats you want

Cancelling combined formats
To return to the original format(s) select the text to be changed then:

1. Hold down Alt and tap Spacebar to cancel the character reformatting
2. Hold down Alt and tap P to cancel the paragraph reformatting

If you have included two types of character reformatting, clearing one type will also clear the other. For example, if you have boldface letters in italics, attempting to clear the emboldening (Alt+Spacebar) will also clear the italics. Similarly, clearing one type of paragraph reformatting (Alt+P) will clear any other type of paragraph reformatting you have used. For example, a centred heading above justified text would become blocked at the left-hand margin if Alt+P was applied to it as well as to the text below.

Memory jogger
The default paragraph settings are single line spacing, blocked left margin and ragged line-endings.

Text creation
1. TYPE Your Own Name
2. Tap Enter 3 times
3. TYPE in the text of Task 15

Amendments
1. Justify the whole document. (Highlight it using Shift+F10)
2. Centre, embolden (boldface) and underline the heading
3. Reformat the name and address in the fourth paragraph in italics
4. Proofread, correct, SAVE and log your work (filename: YourInitials15, *see* Task 4). PRINT it (Task 8)
5. Reformat the characters, but not the paragraphs, to their default style (highlight the whole document and tap Alt+Spacebar). Note that the boldfacing, underlining and italics have disappeared, but not the justification or centring.

Task 15

THE DATA PROTECTION ACT 1984

This Act aims to make public and thereby to control the use of personal data held on all types of computerised equipment. It also covers data held manually which can be identified using a code held on a computer.

Firms or individuals holding such personal data on living people are required to register with the Data Protection Registrar unless the information they hold is only involved in preparing the text of documents. This will tend to exempt users of word processors from registration, but not users of databases containing more than names and addresses.

The Act gives people the chance to view files held on them and to correct any false information they may contain; excluding files held for a wide class of reasons under the heading of 'security'.

Free booklets on the Act are available from the Office of the Data Protection Registrar, Springfield House, Water Lane, WILMSLOW, Cheshire, SK9 5AX.

Task 16

Objective To display the ruler line

Ruler line The ruler line shows the length of the typing line, and also the positions of tabs, indents and the break mark (eg *see* Task 26); but only for the paragraph the cursor is in. It is similar to the scale bar on a typewriter, except that it does not indicate the widths of the margins on each side of the typing line.

1 Tap Esc for Escape
2 Tap O for Options. (Take a deep breath! Don't be afraid of the number of Options)
3 Tap the ↓, Down key once to skip to **show ruler: (No)**. Tap the Spacebar to select **(Yes)**
5 Tap Enter. The ruler line will now be visible at the top of the window whenever Word is loaded. You should keep it switched on. It looks like this:

1 = [· · · · · · · · 1 · · · · · · · · 2 · · · · · · · · 3 · · · · · · · · 4 · · · · · · · · 5 · · · · · · · ·] · · · · · · · · 7 · · · ·

The square brackets '[' and ']', show the ends of the typing line. The ruler line counts characters in 10s however many characters per inch your printer can produce. In other words, the 1, 2, 3... points on the screen only correspond with 1", 2", 3"... on the printed page when 10 pitch (pica) characters are to be printed.

Default margin settings The left and right margins are preset at 1.25" each for a page 8.5" wide. This gives a typing line of 6" in 10 pitch, (or 60 characters). The length and position of the typing line is stated indirectly: by subtracting the sizes of the margins from the width of the page. Because the position the typing line will have on the printed page does not appear onscreen, it is vital to check the sizes of your margins to make sure you get the placing you require; for instance, to line up with a letterhead (*see* Task 18).

Memory jogger The option in round brackets in a command field is the option selected, eg **(Yes)** above.

Text creation
1 TYPE Your Own Name
2 Tap Enter 3 times
3 TYPE in the text of Task 16

Amendments Display the ruler line. Notice that no text extends beyond the square brackets (although sometimes it can).

Proofread, correct, SAVE and log your work (filename: YourInitials16, *see* Task 4). PRINT it (*see* Task 8).

Task 16

FAX (FACSIMILE TRANSMISSION)

Fax is a well-established form of electronic mail whereby any document,
whether it contains handwriting, graphics or photographs, can be
transmitted over the telephone lines to any compatible receiver.

To transmit, the sender dials the number of the receiver, to make sure
it is ready to receive the document, and simply feeds the original into
the machine. The copy, or facsimile, emerges on the receiver's fax
machine, anywhere in the world. The speed of transmission varies from
6 minutes down to a matter of seconds per A4 page, depending on the
type of fax machine used.

There are over a million fax users in the UK, and British Telecom has
published a directory of UK users. Anyone who does not possess a fax
machine of their own can use their local printer or British Telecom's
Bureaufax service which is run from offices up and down the country.

Task 17

Objective To format the page to A4

'Default' defined A 'default' is the setting or choice you get unless you deliberately choose something else. The default page measurements for a new copy of Word are: **page length: 11"**; **page width: 8.5"**. Your machine may already have been set up for the size of paper you are using. To set up an A4 page, or to check whether a set up has been made:

Setting page measurements for A4
1 Tap Esc for Escape
2 Tap F for Format
3 Tap D for Division
4 Tap M for Margins
5 Tap the ↓, Down, key twice to select **page length: 11"**
6 Type in 11.69 for the length of an A4 page
7 Tap the →, Right, key once to select (page) **width: 8.5"**
8 Type 8.27 for its width
9 Tap Enter

Making A4 the default page size
If you usually use A4 paper and print at 10 characters per inch make A4 the default page size. Every **new** document you type will be designed for the A4 page until the default page size is changed again.

1 Display the ruler line if it is not already visible (*see* Task 16)
2 Tap Esc for Escape, F for Format, D for Division, M for Margins, as above
3 Tap the ←, Left, direction key once only to highlight the **use as default: Yes (No)** prompt
4 Tap the Spacebar once to select **(Yes)**
5 Tap Enter

Text creation
1 TYPE Your Own Name
2 Tap Enter 3 times
3 TYPE in the text of Task 17

Amendments
1 Set the page measurements for an A4 page
2 If you usually use A4 paper, print at 10 characters per inch, and if it is appropriate in your circumstances then make A4 the default page size

Proofread, correct, SAVE and log your work (filename: YourInitials17 , *see* Task 4). PRINT it (*see* Task 8).

Task 17

JARGON

There are some unusual words used in word processing and computing.
Here are a few you may not have encountered.

USER-FRIENDLY: computers or programs which are easy to use.

WIMPs: windows, icons, menus and pointers - are different ways of
making programs more user-friendly.

ICONS are pictures representing computer functions. A dustbin, for
instance, might mean delete. There is typically a row of icons
onscreen instead of a menu of named functions.

POINTERS: the arrow which appears on the screen when a mouse is used is
called a pointer.

WYSIWYG ('wisiwig'): what you see is what you get - what you see on the
screen should be printed looking exactly the same.

Task 18

Objective To alter margins

Altering margins	It is generally easier to alter margins before you have typed in a document, especially if you will be setting tabs. This task assumes you have already set the page size to A4 (*see* Task 17).
. . . Before typing	1 Display the ruler line if it is not already visible (*see* Task 16) 2 Tap Esc for Escape 3 Tap F for Format 4 Tap D for Division 5 Tap M for Margins. **FORMAT DIVISION MARGINS** shows options for setting out a printed page 6 Tap the ↓, Down, key once to skip to: **left: 1.25"**. TYPE in the new margin; eg 1 for 1" 7 Tap the →, Right, key once to skip to: **right: 1.25"**. TYPE in the new margin; eg .5 for 0.5" 8 Tap Enter. A division mark is created: a line of colons across the screen. 9 Move the cursor on to or above the division mark 10 Tap Enter several times to move the division mark out of the way further down the screen. This will avoid your deleting it accidentally, or in the apparent disappearance of the cursor as you type. Delete the surplus line spaces when the document is finished
. . . After typing	Follow steps 1–8 above. You have a set typing line of 6.7" (in 10 pitch) or 67 characters across an A4 page. The new margins extend down to the division mark.
Division mark	The division mark stores the formatting for the new margins. You may come across it when you tap Ctrl+Pg Dn to move to the bottom of a document or if you tap Ctrl+Enter by accident. Delete a division mark created accidentally, or to reset the default margins.
Setting new default margins	Re-read the paragraph on '**Default margin settings**' in Task 16. Use the method given in Task 17 to make A4 the default page size and alter the **left:**, **right:**, **top:** and **bottom:** fields.

Memory Jogger To abandon a command tap Esc for Escape (but not for Help, etc, *see* page 3).
Tap Esc for Escape and tap U for Undo, to restore a division mark deleted by accident.

Text creation
1 TYPE Your Own Name
2 Tap Enter 3 times
3 TYPE in the text of Task 18
4 Alter the left margin to 1.0" and the right margin to 0.5", giving a typing line of 6.7"

Amendments Proofread, correct, SAVE and log your work (filename: YourInitials18, *see* Task 4). PRINT it (*see* Task 8).

Task 18

ELECTRONIC MAIL

Sending documents by post can be slow. Telephone lines are often
engaged and call charges can be high. Courier services are very
expensive. With computerisation, communicating with another office in
the same building, or on the other side of the globe, has become much
easier.

Telexes can be prepared during the day and sent out of office hours to
benefit from cheaper call rates.

Desktop computers can be used as electronic mailboxes into which
messages can be posted at a moment's notice for a correspondent to
return to. Security is maintained by passwords.

Automatic re-dialling facilities, which try again and again until a
clear line is available, have simplified many services, including the
transmission of facsimiles.

Some companies give such a high priority to the rapid and secure
transmission of voice, data and documents that they have built private
telecommunications networks in preference to using public systems.

Task 19

Objective   To type wide documents

Wide text

A wide document has a typing line broader than the window's width of nearly 80 characters. Check that your printer can cope with wide text or condensed characters. Type your document directly into the window, where you can see its full width all the time. Reformat it to a typing line wider than the screen afterwards, unless it will include a complicated layout such as tab stops across its full width, when the page width and margins should be set beforehand.

1   Display the ruler line (*see* Task 16)
2   Tap Esc for Escape
3   Tap F for Format
4   Tap D for Division
5   Tap M for Margins
6   Tap the ↓, Down, key twice and the →, Right, key once each to select
     (page) **width: 8.27"**, assuming you have already set the page size to A4 (*see* Task 17)
7   TYPE the new page width, say 12.5 for 12.5" in 10 pitch. This gives a typing line of 10" (page width
     12.5" minus left and right margins of 1.25" each)
8   Tap Enter

Horizontal scrolling

When sideways movement or typing in a wide document reaches the edge of the window the text scrolls horizontally in steps to reveal parts of the typing line which had been offscreen. To view quickly:

Tap →, Right, with the Scroll Lock ON to scroll right ⅓ of a window at a time
Tap ←, Left, with the Scroll Lock ON to scroll left ⅓ of a window at a time

The above keystrokes should be used to view a document's width generally. They are better for this purpose than the Home and End keys because they work even when the typing line containing the cursor is very short. The Home and End keys should be saved for the examination of single lines.

Memory jogger   Switch the Scroll Lock OFF after use to free the ←, Left, and →, Right, direction keys.

Text creation

1   TYPE Your Own Name
2   Tap Enter 3 times
3   TYPE in the text of Task 19 and set a new page width of 12.5" to increase the typing line to 10"

Amendments   Proofread, correct, SAVE and log your work (filename: YourInitials19, *see* Task 4). PRINT it (*see* Task 8).

Task 19

In continental Europe it is quite common for people to speak not merely
one foreign language, but two. An English person who can speak even
one other language fluently is rare.

Foreign companies complain about dealing with British companies whose
sales literature is all in English and whose representatives speak only
English.

Whilst the attention paid to foreign languages in this country is
increasing, it is nothing like the importance of English abroad. Half
the world's scientific literature is printed in English. English is
the main language in computer technology, aviation, shipping and sport.

For an office worker in the UK this is not a reason for complacency,
but a source of opportunity. With English as one's own tongue, the
addition of another language offers scope for more interesting and
enjoyable work.

Task 20

Objective	To display and use the paragraph and new line formatting marks

---

Formatting marks	The invisible formatting marks contain instructions for the formatting of text, as does the division mark. When visible, they make it easier to control the typing of text with complicated layouts, such as tables.
Displaying formatting marks	1 Tap Esc for Escape 2 Tap O for Options 3 Tap the →, Right, key once and the ↓, Down, key once to select: **show non-printing symbols: (None) Partial All**. Tap P to select (**Partial**) 4 Tap Enter. This command displays the paragraph mark and the new line mark. They are never printed. They will be displayed until a different option is chosen
Paragraph mark (¶)	The paragraph mark is typed at the end of a paragraph whenever you tap Enter. It contains paragraph (not character) formatting instructions for the paragraph that precedes it, eg tab stops or justification.
New line mark (↓)	The new line mark is typed at the end of a line when you hold down Shift and tap Enter. This keystroke is called tapping New line. It starts a new line without ending one paragraph and starting a new one. It is vital to tap New line at the ends of lines in tables. (*See* **Memory jogger** also.)
Accidental deletion of a paragraph mark	**Beware** accidentally deleting the paragraph mark, especially when typing a table. You will lose your tab stops and your table may collapse into a jumble of words! If this happens tap Escape, Undo at once. The solution is always to tap New line and **not** Enter at the end of each line within the table. Only tap Enter to end the table.

Memory jogger	It is useful to tap New line after sub-headings (eg after shoulder headings, *see* Task 20 below) and after short lines to be selected as a single block of text, eg a list (*see* Task 4), or the inside address of a letter.
Text creation	1 TYPE Your Own Name 2 Tap Enter 3 times 3 Prepare the window to display the paragraph and new line marks 4 TYPE in the text of Task 20. Tap Enter twice after 'Task 20' but tap New line twice after the shoulder headings 'SOFTWARE', 'HARDWARE' etc
Amendments	1 Move the paragraph on 'HARDWARE' above 'SOFTWARE'. Leave one line space between paragraphs 2 Justify the paragraph on 'SOFTWARE'. Delete its paragraph mark. Notice that it takes on the formatting contained in the paragraph mark that follows it. Tap Enter once to insert a line 3 Proofread, correct, SAVE and log your work (filename: YourInitials20, *see* Task 4). PRINT it (Task 8).

Task 20

If you are thinking about buying a microcomputer have you really worked out what you want it for, or if you really need it? If you have, it is wise to consider the following points before spending any money on computer equipment.

SOFTWARE

There should be a range of good software for the machine you are interested in. In fact, since you buy a computer to solve problems, and not just to look good on a desk, the software available might be more important to you than the particular machine bought.

HARDWARE

The computer should have a large enough memory (RAM) for the programs you want to run on it, and operate fast enough for your needs and temperament.

EXPANDABILITY

Can you easily and comparatively cheaply upgrade the system as your needs grow? For example, can you add on a hard disk, a high-resolution screen or a telex unit?

EASE OF USE

Is the computer and are the programs user-friendly? If not, you will have to spend a lot more time and effort using them than is necessary.

Task 21

Objective	To set and move tabs

Setting tabs
1. Set the ruler line and display the new line and paragraph formatting marks (*see* Tasks 16 and 20)
2. Tap Esc for Escape
3. Tap F for Format
4. Tap T for Tabs
5. Tap S for Set
6. TYPE in the measurement of the tab you want to set
7. To set several tabs (with the same alignment) tap Ins for Insert after typing each measurement. When the last tab has been set:
8. Tap Enter. Setting a new tab stop clears all the default tab stops to its left. A letter 'L' for Left alignment appears in the ruler line. This means the column at that tab will be blocked at its left
9. SAVE your work before continuing (filename: YourInitials21, *see* Task 4)

If a tab has been inserted wrongly, or to make the spaces between the columns equal, move the tab(s).

Moving tabs
1. Move the cursor into the line/table where tabs are to be moved. Follow steps 1–5 above
2. Tap F1, then use the ↓, Down, and ↑, Up, direction keys to move to the tabs you want to move
3. Tap Ctrl+←, to move the tab stop to a new position to the left and
   Tap Ctrl+→, to move the tab stop to a new position to the right. If you pass over a tab stop as you move to the left or right, that tab stop will be deleted
4. Repeat Step 3 for all the tab stops you want to move
5. Tap Enter

Text creation
1. TYPE Your Own Name
2. Tap Enter 3 times
3. TYPE in the text of Task 21 up to and including the word 'keyboards'. Tap Enter twice
4. Set tabs at 1.4" and 3.4". Re-read **Accidental deletion of a paragraph mark** in Task 20
5. TYPE in the remainder of Task 21, observing correct column discipline, ie tap New line (which means Shift+Enter) at the end of each line of the table and in each clear line space also
6. At the end of the last line only, tap Enter to finish the table as one paragraph (*see* Task 20)
7. Move the tab at 3.4" to 3.1" to make the spaces between the columns equal

Amendments
Proofread, correct, SAVE and log your work (filename: YourInitials21, *see* Task 4). PRINT it (*see* Task 8).

Task 21

'THE CURSORS' - Concerts This Autumn

Featuring: AL TAPPER on keyboards

Date	Venue	Tickets (£)
1 Sept	Manchester	3.50 - 12.50
10 Sept	Bristol	2.50 - 10.50
21 Sept	Cardiff	2.50 - 10.50
1 Oct	London	4.00 - 15.00

Task 22

Objective	To clear tabs and reset the default tabs

Clearing one tab	1	Tap [Esc] for Escape
	2	Tap [F] for Format
	3	Tap [T] for Tabs
	4	Tap [C] for Clear. (This displays the ruler line even if you have not done so already.)
	5	TYPE in the [measurement] of the tab stop you want to clear (eg [5], for a tab at 5")
	6	Tap [Enter]
Clearing several tabs	1	Follow steps 1–5 above
	2	TYPE a comma [,] immediately after the first measurement. Do not type in a space
	3	TYPE the [measurement] of the second tab to be cleared
	4	Tap [Enter] if this is the last tab to be cleared. If it is not, TYPE another comma [,]. Do not type a space
	5	Repeat the procedure until the positions of all the unwanted tabs are recorded, separated by commas only
	6	Tap [Enter]
Clearing all tabs	1	Tap [Esc] for Escape
	2	Tap [F] for Format
	3	Tap [T] for Tabs
	4	Tap [R] for Reset-all tabs. All new tabs disappear and the invisible default tabs are reset every 0.5"

Memory jogger	Undo the clearing of tabs in the usual way (by pressing [Esc] for Escape and tapping [U] for Undo)

Text creation	1	Load the text of the file [YourInitials21] (see Task 5). Display the ruler line and the formatting marks. If you typed the heading 'Task 21' change it to 'Task 22'
	2	Move the cursor to the paragraph mark (¶) at the end of the last line of the table
	3	Tap [Enter] 3 times
	4	Clear all tabs
	5	TYPE in the text of Task 22 (omitting 'Task 22') from 'STOP PRESS' to 'all-inclusive prices'
	6	Set new tabs at 1.8", 3.1", 4.4", 5" and 5.5" on the ruler line and type in the rest of the task
	7	Clear the tabs at 5" and 5.5"

Amendments	Proofread, correct, SAVE and log your work (filename: [YourInitials22], see Task 4). PRINT it (see Task 8).

Task 22

STOP PRESS!

Accommodation now available at reduced rates.

For the Bristol, Cardiff and London venues Happy Sleeper motels are offering rooms for the night of the concert and breakfast the next morning, at all-inclusive prices.

	Bristol	Cardiff	London
Single rooms	£26.50	£26.50	£33.00
Double rooms (per person)	£23.50	£23.50	£25.00

Every room has a private bathroom, colour TV, telephone and tea/coffee making facilities.

Task 23

Objective   To move columns

Column discipline

1. When you type columns of text you may wish to move, tap the `Tab` key once between each column and at the end of each line of the table. It will then be possible to move **any** column as a block of text. (If you tried to swap the last column of a table without doing so you would jumble up your text)
2. Tap `New line`, (`Shift+Enter`), at the end of every line of a table starting at the first line of column headings, if any, and include any clear lines within a table (eg the clear lines in the Table of Task 20)
3. Tap `ENTER` **only** at the end of the last line. This safely ends the table as a paragraph (*see* Task 19)

Moving columns

A column is highlighted like any block of text and then moved. It is vital to follow good column discipline when typing the text of columns that will be moved.

1. Display the formatting marks: `Esc`ape, `O`ptions, move to **show non-printing symbols:** Tap `A` for (**All**) then `Enter`. Two new symbols will appear in typed text: '→' for the Tab key and '·' for the Spacebar 'spaces'
2. Place the cursor on the first character of the first word at the top of the column to be moved (eg the G of GENERAL in Task 23 below)
3. Hold down `Shift` and tap `F6`. The letters **CS** (Column Select) appear in the Status Line
4. Use the arrowed direction keys to highlight the whole column including the tab arrows, '→'
5. Tap `Esc` for Escape
6. Tap `D` for Delete. This deletes the column to the Scrap
7. Move the cursor to the new position for the column to begin (eg the W of WORD PROCESSING in Task 23 below). Always move the deleted column at once, otherwise you may lose it from the Scrap.
8. Tap `Ins` for Insert. Move the tab stops to make the spaces between the columns equal (*see* Task 21)

Text creation

1. TYPE `Your Own Name`
2. Tap `Enter` 3 times
3. Set left and right margins at 0.5". TYPE in the text of Task 23, setting tabs at 2.4" and 4.8" (*see* Task 21)
4. Proofread, correct, SAVE and log your work (filename: `YourInitials23`, *see* Task 4). PRINT it (Task 8)

Amendments

1. Make the column headed GENERAL the first column of your table
2. Move the column headed WORD PROCESSING below the table, beneath the first column
3. Move the WORD PROCESSING 'column' back into the table as the first column
4. SAVE and log your work (filename: `YourInitials23A`, *see* Task 4). PRINT it (*see* Task 8).

Task 23

WORDS, WORDS, WORDS

As a word processor operator you have already met, and will continue to
meet, many terms used in information processing. If you are unfamiliar
with any of the words in the following lists, find out what they mean.

WORD PROCESSING	COMMUNICATIONS	GENERAL
automatic backup	answerback	accounting packages
background printing	acoustic coupler	compatibility
boilerplating	baud rate	databases
borders (boxes)	bridge	DOS
cross-training	bulletin boards	feasibility study
footers	confirmed delivery	graphics
glossary	Dialcom (BT)	hacker
grammar checker	error handling	housekeeping
headers	gateway	integrated software
mailmerge	Intelpost	interfaces
multicolumn style	mailbox	languages
originator	money transfer	laptop
outlining	on-line information	OCR
purge	PABX	read-write head
sheet feeder	Prestel	security
spelling checker	PSS (BT)	spreadsheets
style sheet	Telecom Gold	systems analyst
template	teleconferencing	windowing
thesaurus	videotext	write-protect notch
vertical tab stop	wide area network	zooming

Task 24

Objective	To use fully blocked and inset paragraphs

Blocked and inset paragraphs
Blocked paragraphs are the default paragraph style. Every line starts at the left-hand margin. Inset paragraphs start some distance in from either or both margins. They may be blocked, indented or hanging. It is easier to inset after typing than before. The instructions below describe insetting in steps of the default tab width of 0.5". To inset from the left margin or from both margins:

. . . After typing

1 Select the paragraph(s) to be inset:

2 **Left margin only:** hold down [Alt] and tap [N] once for each step of 0.5" (the default tab width)
  Both margins:　　hold down [Alt] and tap [Q] once for each step of 0.5" (the default tab width)

The degree of insetting of a paragraph is shown in the ruler line by the left square bracket '[' being inset to the same extent

. . . Before typing

1 Tap [Enter] at the end of the text which will precede the inset text. Repeat step 2 above
2 TYPE in the text to be inset, tapping [Enter] at the end of each paragraph

Reducing and cancelling insetting

1 Select the appropriate paragraph(s)
2 Hold down [Alt] and tap [M] once for each 0.5" reduction in insetting from the left margin

Other paragraph formats which may apply to the paragraph(s) will be unaffected. If you hold down [Alt] and tap [P] for Plain paragraph format, then all paragraph formats will be cancelled (*see* Task 14).

To check how much a paragraph is inset move the cursor into that paragraph and look at the ruler line.

Memory joggers
The cursor must be within a paragraph for the ruler line to reveal its formatting (as far as it can). [New line], ie [Shift+Enter] starts a new line without starting a new paragraph.

Text creation

1 TYPE [Your Own Name]
2 Tap [Enter] 3 times
3 TYPE in the text of Task 24, insetting the quotations 0.5" from the left-hand margin and typing them line for line as shown below. Tap [New line] at the ends of the first lines of the two-line quotes

Amendments
Proofread your work and correct any errors you find. SAVE your work using the filename:
[YourInitials24] (*see* Task 4) and record its details in your manual log of files. PRINT it (*see* Task 8).

Task 24

Some plays just 'run and run': Shakespeare's works for instance. And
they were written nearly 400 years ago! Although frequently the butt
of the jokes of modern comedians, his works are as powerful today to
move and command respect as they were then.

Some fragments are known to nearly everyone, but not always who said
them and in which play. Can you identify these quotes?

'O Romeo, Romeo! Wherefore art thou Romeo?'

'But soft! What light through yonder window breaks?
It is the east, and Juliet is the sun.'

Two easy ones to start with. Now try:

'To be, or not to be - that is the question;'

and:

'Friends, Romans, countrymen, lend me your ears;
I come to bury Caesar, not to praise him.'

Finally:

'Once more unto the breach, dear friends, once more;
Or close the wall up with our English dead.'

Task 25

Objective To inset text (continued)

Insetting other distances To inset text distances other than in steps of the default tab stops a more lengthy procedure is needed than shown in Task 24. It is generally easier to inset text after you have typed in a document.

. . . After typing
1 Highlight (select) the text to be inset from either one or from both margins (*see* Task 10)
2 Tap `Esc` for Escape
3 Tap `F` for Format
4 Tap `P` for Paragraph
5 Tap the `↓`, `Down`, key once to select **left indent:**
6 TYPE the size of the indent; eg `.75` for 0.75" in 10 pitch. To indent from:
7 **The left margin only:** tap `Enter`; then tap a cursor (direction) key to cancel the highlight
   Both margins: tap the `→`, `Right`, key twice to select **right indent:**
8 TYPE the right indent required; eg `.75` for 0.75" (to give an even indent from both sides in this case)
9 Tap `Enter`. The highlighted text will be inset 0.75" from both the left and right margins. Square brackets in the ruler line indicate the new length of the typing line in the reformatted paragraph(s)
10 Tap a cursor (direction) key to cancel the highlight

. . . Before typing
1 Follow steps 2–7 above to indent from the left margin; and steps 2–10 to indent from both margins
2 When you have finished typing the inset part of your document tap `Enter` to finish the paragraph
3 Hold down `Alt` and tap `P` for Plain paragraph format (*see* Task 14). TYPE the rest of the document

Memory jogger If you are typing in text with short lines, eg an address, use `New line` (`Shift+Enter`) at the end of each line except the last, when you should tap `Enter`. This text is now a complete paragraph and when using F9 or F10, all the short lines will become highlighted with one keystroke (*see* Task 10).

Text creation
1 TYPE `Your Own Name`
2 Tap `Enter` 3 times
3 TYPE in the text of Task 25

Amendments
1 Give the task a heading 'NETWORKS'
2 Highlight the second and third paragraphs and inset them 0.75" from both margins

Proofread, correct, SAVE and log your work (filename: `YourInitials25`, *see* Task 4). PRINT it (*see* Task 8).

Task 25

A network is a number of computers and/or other electronic devices
connected by cable or by telecommunications via a telephone line. Most
networks are local area networks (or LANs). They may cover a classroom
or a whole building. Individual workstations in the network can be used
on different tasks at the same time and users benefit from sharing
centrally held programs, datafiles and storage (memory) facilities. A
network is likely to include at least one printer and may be able to
communicate with other networks or electronic devices located far away.

To avoid the chaos that would arise if, for example, several users
wanted to print at the same time, the resources of a network may be
controlled by 'servers'. Thus printing would be controlled by a print
server; a file server would control loading and saving files. Servers
may be combined in one microcomputer dedicated to controlling these
tasks alone. If you are working in a classroom with a network, is there
one workstation which the teacher uses at the start and end of the
lesson, but which is otherwise unused? This is probably the server.

Networks can be set up to send and receive text by electronic mail and
telex (Task 18) or by facsimile transmission (Task 16). More
exotically, they can be used for voice conferencing or to gain access to
mainframe computers. This means you could sit at your workstation and
'talk' to a computer on the other side of the world.

For computers to 'talk' to each other when miles apart what they have to
'say' has to be sent along a telephone line. Unfortunately computers
don't 'talk' in a way which the telephone system can understand.
Therefore translators, or 'modems', are connected to both of the
computers to translate the signals at each end of the telephone line.

Task 26

Objective	To use indented and hanging paragraphs

. . . Before typing	Since documents prepared with either indented or hanging paragraphs tend to be consistently of the one style, it is as easy to set up the format before typing as it is to do it afterwards.
Indented paragraphs	Hold down Alt and tap F for First line indent and TYPE in the text.
	The first line only is indented 0.5", ie the default tab width, from the left-hand margin (in 10 pitch). The ruler line indicates the first line indent by a break mark, ' ¦ ', at the 0.5" point.
Hanging paragraphs	Hold down Alt and tap T once only and TYPE in the text.
	The first line only **starts** at the left-hand margin. Subsequent lines are indented 0.5" (the default tab width). (Word calls hanging paragraphs 'hanging indents'). The ruler line shows a break mark ' ¦ ' at the left-hand margin and a '[' at the 0.5" point. Press Alt+T again to indent a further 0.5". Reduce the indent by Alt+M (*see* Task 24).
. . . After typing	Highlight the paragraph(s) to be reformatted and make the appropriate keystrokes as shown above.
Cancelling paragraph styles	1 Select (highlight) the paragraph(s) to be returned to the default style (ie the fully blocked style)
	2 Hold down Alt and tap P for Plain paragraph format

Memory jogger	You can give many commands **before** or **after** typing in text. Try to become flexible in your approach.
Text creation	1 TYPE Your Own Name
	2 Tap Enter 3 times
	3 TYPE in the text of Task 26. Tap Enter twice after the first paragraph
	4 TYPE the rest of the task in the hanging paragraph style, tapping Enter twice after each paragraph
Amendments	1 Proofread, correct, SAVE and log your work (filename: YourInitials26, *see* Task 4). PRINT it (Task 8)
	2 Reformat all the paragraphs, but not the heading, in the indented style. Remember to cancel the hanging paragraph format first. Centre the heading and underline it (*see* Tasks 14 and 13 respectively)
	3 PRINT a copy (*see* Task 8)
	4 Clear the screen (*see* Task 4).

Task 26

PROGRAMS

The world's computer market is awash with software programs for every
kind of application. (Notice that 'programs' is spelt differently from
the 'programmes' you may watch on TV). On personal computers some of
the most common application programs are:

(1)   WORD PROCESSORS From basic letter-writers to sophisticated
      desktop publishing systems, WP programs specialise in the
      manipulation of text and graphics.

(2)   SPREADSHEETS These are grids on which calculations may be
      performed with great ease: after the spreadsheet has been set up!
      Setting up may involve a range of difficulty, from adding
      columns of figures to give simple totals, to a mind-boggling
      series of linked formulas. A spreadsheet can be recalculated
      immediately even if only one figure changes, or if many change at
      the same time. This means that a business can easily work out
      what would happen if its sales, purchases, wages etc were all to
      change at different rates, with some going up and some going down.

(3)   DATABASES (or database management systems - DBMS) Imagine a
      record card with boxes for different kinds of information: name,
      address, telephone number, age, sex, estimated income, credit-
      worthiness. A DBMS can store, retrieve, update and compare this
      information on millions of 'record cards' so that it can be used
      for business purposes. Direct mail selling frequently uses
      database information to try and sell only to those people whom the
      seller thinks are the most likely to give him a sale.

Task 27

Objective   Formatting line endings: hyphens and the hard space

Long words wrapped around to a new line can spoil a document's right-hand side. Hyphenating them may overcome this problem. There are 3 types of hyphen: ordinary, soft and hard (or 'non-breaking').

Ordinary hyphen   Tap the Hyphen key (-) once. The ordinary hyphen is used between words that are hyphenated wherever they appear in a line and when those words would be split by a line-ending at the hyphen-point: eg well-known, time-consuming, up-to-date.

Soft hyphen   Hold down Ctrl and tap the Hyphen key (-) once.
Use the soft hyphen in words which would not be hyphenated if they fell in the middle of a line. The hyphen is 'soft' because it disappears when reformatting moves the 'hyphenated' word to the middle of a line. More than one soft hyphen can be inserted into a word, as in 'communications' in Task 27 below.

Hard hyphen   Hold down Ctrl and Shift together and tap the Hyphen key (-) once.
The hard hyphen is used in words or figures which should not be separated by a line-ending even though they contain hyphens: a name like Templeton-Brown, for instance; or 1939–45 or −5 degrees C.

Hard space   Hold down Ctrl and tap the Spacebar once. Use it to prevent words splitting at line-endings.
Eg between '10' on one line and 'pm' on the next, a hard space would put '10 pm' on one line.

Text creation
1   Set the typing line to 6" (60 characters). (Left margin 1.25"; right margin 1" on an A4 page: Task 18)
2   TYPE Your Own Name
3   Tap Enter 3 times
4   TYPE in the text of Task 27. Only type in the ordinary hyphens shown

Amendments
1   Hyphenate 'communications' using soft hyphens in 3 places successively: 'com-muni-ca-tions'. Watch how the word wraps back to the previous line. (If your soft hyphens are visible tap: Esc ape, O ptions, →, (Right), ↓, (Down)). At the prompt **show non-printing symbols:** tap N (for None)
2   Notice that the name 'Templeton-Brown' has now split at the end of a line
3   Delete the ordinary hyphen in 'Templeton-Brown' and insert a hard hyphen
4   Justify the whole document. (Tap a direction key to clear the highlight)
Proofread, correct, SAVE and log your work (filename: YourInitials27, see Task 4). PRINT it (see Task 8).

Task 27

At last week's meeting of the Computer Buffs Club, the vice-chairman, Mr Braithwaite, introduced the visiting speaker as usual. On this occasion it was the well-known communications specialist from New Zealand, Mr William Templeton-Brown.

He lectured on the subject of microcomputers and electronic mail, using film clips and slides to good effect. He suggested several ways in which a group such as the Club could reduce the time members have to spend trying to keep up-to-date with the latest developments.

Task 28

Objective	To use the search facility

Search	1 Hold down Ctrl and tap Pg Up (for example) to move above the area of text to be searched 2 Tap Esc for Escape 3 Tap S for Search 4 TYPE in the text you want to find, the **SEARCH text** 5 Tap Enter

The cursor now selects (highlights) the first instance of the search text in the document below its starting position which meets the requirements of the two default conditions, **case: (No)** and **whole word: (No)**. It will highlight instances which are both whole words themselves and parts of other words, and in both upper and lower case letters. (Eg if 'Painting' existed in the document and the search text: was 'paint', the 'Paint' in 'Painting' would be selected even though it has an initial capital and is part of another word.)

To search for text: above the cursor (omit step 1 above and)   select: **direction: (Up)**
of the same case (or mix of cases) as the search text   select: **case: (Yes)**
including whole words only   select: **whole word: (Yes)**

Repeat search	Hold down Shift and tap the F4 key once. This finds the next instance of the search text.

The message **Search text not found** indicates that the search is over. The cursor is left on the last instance found, if the search was successful, or where it started if the search failed.

Text creation	1 TYPE Your Own Name 2 Tap Enter 3 times 3 TYPE in the text of Task 28
Amendments	1 Find every instance of paint using the two default conditions stated above. Count them. (5 instances) 2 Hold down Ctrl and tap Pg Dn. Repeat the search of Amendment 1, but select **direction: (Up)** 3 Hold down Ctrl and tap Pg Up. Find every instance of Paint whether or not it forms part of a whole word. Select **case: (Yes)** and **direction: (Down)**. (2 instances) 4 Find every instance of Paint again, but only whole words. Select **whole word: (Yes)**. Repeat search for Paint. (1 instance only. The occurrence of 'Paint' within 'Painting' is omitted)

Proofread, correct, SAVE and log your work (filename: YourInitials28, *see* Task 4). PRINT it (*see* Task 8).

Task 28

The mouse is a hand-held device connected to a computer which can be used in conjunction with a keyboard. Its shape resembles a mouse with a cable for a tail and buttons for eyes. The operator's hand rests on top of the mouse with the first and second fingers over its 'eyes'.

Sliding the mouse over the desk top beside the computer rotates a direction-sensitive ball inside it which in turn moves a pointer over the screen.

Commands are chosen from an onscreen menu by touching them with the tip of the pointer and executed by pressing one or both of the buttons.

On colour monitors, the pointer can be used as a paintbrush. Paint is represented by red, blue, green and other squares of colour at the side of the screen. Pictures are created by dipping the pointer into the colours and painting-in the screen as desired. Thick or thin lines of paint or a sprayed effect can be obtained. Painting is also possible on some screens using a light-pen.

Task 29

Objective	To use the replace facility

Replace

Words or phrases may be replaced either throughout the length of a document in one step, or optionally at each occurrence. Replacements are made below the cursor or within a selected block of text.

1 Move the cursor above the text to be replaced or select a block of text which contains it
2 Tap Esc for Escape
3 Tap R for Replace
4 TYPE in the text to be replaced beside the prompt **REPLACE text:**
5 Tap the →, Right, key once to move to the **with text:** prompt
6 TYPE in the text you want to put in its place
7 Tap Enter. The cursor moves to the first occurrence of the **REPLACE text** typed in below its starting position or within the highlighted text. It will highlight text in both upper or lower case letters, and whether or not any of the text to be replaced forms part of another word. To replace it:
8 Tap Y for Yes, to replace; tap N for No to skip and continue, or tap Esc for Escape to finish

To replace text: throughout the document in one step ('without confirmation') select: **confirm: (No)**
of the same case as the text to be replaced select: **case: (Yes)**
which only includes whole words select: **whole word: (Yes)**

When replacing is complete, the cursor returns to its starting position, unless the command was cancelled. The number of replacements made appears in the Message Line.

Memory jogger

To cancel a command before completing it, tap Esc for Escape.

Text creation

1 TYPE Your Own Name
2 Tap Enter 3 times
3 TYPE in the text of Task 29

Amendments

1 Move the cursor to the top of the document (hold down Ctrl and tap Pg Up)
2 Replace the word work with employment. Use the **confirm: (Yes)** and the **whole word: (Yes)** options (6 instances, including the heading)
3 Third paragraph: replace the word backing with support. Use the **confirm: (No)** option. (1 instance)

Proofread, correct, SAVE and log your work (filename: YourInitials29, *see* Task 4). PRINT it (*see* Task 8).

Task 29

THE FUTURE OF WORK

The cheapness and power of the latest computer and communications
systems provide opportunities for new ways of organising work.

One view of the future of work is that large firms will not employ the
enormous numbers of people they employ today. Instead they will be
made up of a small professional core supplemented by part-timers plus
a number of small firms to which they will contract out work.

The ability to communicate cheaply over long distances will reduce the
need for workers to commute to offices. They will be able to work from
home using the firm's computer equipment. This may involve self-
employment with a measure of backing from the firm.

Companies dispersed in this way will tend to use local firms more than
they do today, reinforcing a trend towards small-scale enterprises. In
fact, it is expected that most of the growth in work will come, not
from big firms, still less from manufacturing, but from new small
firms. These firms will offer personal services: services that are
less likely to be subject to automation.

It is unlikely that people training for work today will be prepared for
a job for life. Instead they will have to retrain in future, perhaps
to do jobs they cannot even imagine today.

Experiments and trends in these directions are visible now. Some say
they are the 'shape of things to come'.

Task 30

Objective   Using the search facility to complete a standard letter

Preparation of standard letter	TYPE the text of the letter, inserting a symbol (eg '@') at the points where variable details are to be inserted. SAVE it using a distinctive filename extension such as '.ltr' (*see* Task 4).
Completion of standard letter	**A** Retrieve the blank standard letter, loading it using the method given in Task 5.
	B Fill in the details:

1. Tap `Esc` for Escape
2. Tap `S` for Search (*see* Task 28). In response to the prompt: **SEARCH text:**
3. TYPE in `@`
4. Tap `Enter`. The cursor will move to the first occurrence of '@'
5. Delete the '@' symbol and TYPE in the details to be inserted there
6. Hold down `Shift` and tap `F4` to move the cursor to the next occurrence of '@'
7. Repeat steps 5 and 6 until the letter has been completed
8. SAVE the completed letter as a document '.doc' file (*see* the text of Task 5 on FILENAME EXTENSIONS). The original version of the letter is still saved for future retrieval and completion
9. PRINT a copy to send, and one for your file (if appropriate)

Memory joggers   Check that Overtype (OT) is off. Switch off other locking keys shown in the Status Line (*see* page 5). To locate a file in the directory, containing the .LTR filename extension, tap `Esc` for Escape, tap `T` for Transfer, tap `L` for Load, TYPE `*.Ltr` and tap `F1` (*see* Task 6).

Text creation

1. TYPE `Your Own Name`
2. Tap `Enter` 3 times
3. TYPE in the text of Task 30. Turn to page 68 for the lower half of the letter
4. Proofread and correct your work
5. SAVE it using the filename: `YourInitials30.ltr` (*see* Task 4) and record its details in your manual log (*see* the text of Task 6)
6. PRINT a copy to keep for reference
7. Carry out the **Amendments** overleaf (page 67).

Task 30

W I L L I A M S '   W I N E S
"Our only returns are empties"

REF: JBW/Your Initials

Today's date

@

Dear @

Thank you for your order for @ of self-opening wine bottles. We can
supply them from stock and shall be despatching them to you within the
next few days.

Unfortunately, due to the recent industrial dispute involving the road
haulage industry, it is taking longer than usual for orders to reach
our customers. We therefore regret that your goods will probably take
six weeks to arrive instead of a month. However, our carriers assure
us that their services will be back to normal within a fortnight.

Continued

Task 30 (continued)

Amendments

1 TYPE into the letter the details shown in box **a** below, as follows:

first @: the name and address
second @: the title and surname
third @: the number of cases of bottles

2 Check your entries. SAVE the letter using the filename YourInitials30a (*see* Task 4) and PRINT one copy (*see* Task 8)
3 Clear the screen (*see* Task 4)
4 Retrieve another blank letter
5 Complete a second letter using the details in box **b** below. SAVE it (filename: YourInitials30b) and PRINT one copy. Clear the screen
6 Complete a third letter in the same way using the details in box **c** below. SAVE it using the filename YourInitials30c and PRINT one copy. Clear the screen.

a

```
Mrs K Martin
28 Reynolds Avenue
BOVINGFORD
Lincs BW5 8RT
Mrs Martin
6 cases
```

b

```
Mr L G Lyddon
81 Chesterfield Road
LONDON N14 4LT
Mr Lyddon
18 cases
```

c

```
Miss M E Miles
4 Long Lane
ILBOROUGH
Tyne and Wear
IL6 7TZ
Miss Miles
10 cases
```

Please find enclosed details of the exciting new range of wine-making equipment we are introducing. As you will see, we are offering very favourable terms to our regular customers. Since we anticipate strong demand for this new product range we recommend you to place your first order as soon as possible.

Do not hesitate to contact me if I can help you personally.

Yours sincerely

J B Williams
Distribution Manager

Encs

Task 31

Objective

Objective　　　　To merge documents

Merging

The entire text and formatting of one document can be inserted into another as if it were a block of text being inserted from elsewhere in the same document (*see* Task 12).

1　TYPE in a document or load a file (*see* Task 5)
2　Move the cursor to the place where the second document is to be inserted
3　Tap Esc for Escape
4　Tap T for Transfer
5　Tap M for Merge. In response to the prompt: **TRANSFER MERGE filename:**
6　TYPE the filename of the document to be merged
7　Tap Enter

It is usually necessary to tidy up the line spacing when two documents have been merged.

Memory jogger　　Clear the screen before starting a new task. (Tap, one after the other, Escape, Transfer, Clear, Window.)

Text creation　　TYPE in the text of Task 17 now if you have not done so already. *See* **Text creation** in Task 17. SAVE it using the filename: YourInitials17 . Clear the screen before going on to Step 1 below.

1　TYPE Your Own Name
2　Tap Enter 3 times
3　TYPE in the text of Task 31 in the hanging paragraph style (hold down Alt and tap T before typing)
4　Proofread your work correcting any errors you find

Amendments

1　Move the cursor onto the 'B' of 'BYTE' in the first paragraph
2　MERGE the text of Task 17 at this point. The **TRANSFER MERGE filename** should be YourInitials17 . Ensure that there is one line space between the paragraph starting 'BYTE' and the one above it
3　Move to the top of the document by holding down Ctrl and tapping Pg Up
4　Delete the second occurrence of your own name and the heading 'Task 17' (if you had typed in this heading originally). Reformat the second to the sixth paragraphs in the hanging paragraph style
5　Ensure that there is one clear line space between the heading 'Task 31' and the title 'JARGON'

SAVE your work and log its details (filename: YourInitials31 , *see* Task 4). PRINT a copy (*see* Task 8).

Task 31

BYTE: the amount of memory a computer needs to describe one character
of text, data or a program. Because a byte is very small, memory
size is usually spoken of in terms of thousands or millions of
bytes (kilobytes or megabytes respectively).

NLQ: near letter-quality. High quality dot matrix printing which looks
nearly as good as material which has been typed.

WIDOWS & ORPHANS: a widow is the first line of a paragraph left alone
at the foot of a page and an orphan is the last line of a
paragraph carried over to the top of a new page.

INSERT & OVERTYPE are text editing modes. In insert mode, typing into
an existing block of text pushes the old text aside and adds to
it. Typing in overtype mode writes over existing text, deleting
it in the process. With Word, overtype mode is switched on by
tapping F5 once, causing the letters 'OT' to appear in the Status
Line.

Task 32

<table>
<tr><td>**Objective**</td><td colspan="2">To set, move and force page breaks</td></tr>
</table>

Setting page breaks	1	Tap `Esc` for Escape
	2	Tap `P` for Print
	3	Tap `R` for Repaginate. If you are willing to accept the default page breaks
	4	Tap `Enter`. A row of spaced full stops across the screen indicates the page break
Moving page breaks	1	Follow steps 1–3 above
	2	Tap the `Spacebar` once to select **PRINT REPAGINATE confirm page breaks: (Yes)**
	3	Tap `Enter`. The message **Enter Y to confirm page break or use direction keys to reposition** appears*
	4	Move the cursor `↑`, `Up`, and `↓`, `Down`, to the line at which the new page is to start. You cannot move the cursor below the line where **PRINT REPAGINATE** takes it
	5	Tap `Y`. A page break, represented by a dotted line, is set above the line the cursor is in
	6	Repeat steps 4 and 5 for each page break. Cancelling the command leaves page breaks you have set intact
	*	The message **Enter Y to confirm or R to remove page break** appears when the cursor is moved to each page break which had previously been forced or moved from the default setting.
Forcing and removing page breaks	1	Move the cursor to the line where the new page is to start
	2	Hold down `Ctrl` and `Shift` together and tap `Enter`
	3	To remove the forced page break: highlight it and tap the `Del` for Delete key once
Page length		The default page length is 58 lines in an A4 page (70 lines). Top and bottom margins are both 1".

Text creation	1	TYPE `Your Own Name`
	2	Tap `Enter` 3 times
	3	TYPE in the text of Task 32. Reformat the whole document into double line spacing (`Shift+F10`, `Alt+2`)
Amendments	1	Force a page break with the cursor located on the first letter of the first paragraph
	2	Set the page breaks without confirmation. Now set them again using **confirm page breaks: (Yes)**
	3	Confirm the forced page break
	4	Start a third page at the top of the third paragraph by moving the page break upwards

Proofread, correct, SAVE and log your work (filename: `YourInitials32`, *see* Task 4). PRINT it (*see* Task 8).

Task 32

Many companies around the world are developing machines which can respond to, store and replay, synthesise and recognise speech. Built-in computers are the brains behind them. There are machines which will act on a spoken command. Spoken messages can be stored in electronic mailboxes and retrieved by telephone, and by several people at the same time - because the messages are not recorded as on a tape recorder, but on electronic pulses in the computer's memory.

Voice operation has spread furthest where the problems encountered by developers are least difficult to solve. It is comparatively easy to make a machine respond to a simple sound; such as is needed to enter numbers on a spreadsheet. The same is true of storing and playing back voices.

The greatest barrier to full voice operation is the difficulty of achieving voice recognition. The difference between a machine which responds to mere sound and one which responds to the spoken language is like the difference between the speaking clock and the operator in the telephone system. The former reads a prepared script whenever the number is dialled and can do no more. The latter makes up what she says on the spot depending on the enquiry. She can do this because she understands what the enquirer is saying.

It takes a lot of computing power to achieve even a semblance of human understanding. This has held back the development of voice operation. However, computers which process information much faster than before, and programming techniques which emulate the way language works are developing rapidly. They are jointly overcoming the key problem in voice recognition: the great complexity of the spoken language.

Task 33

Objective	To number pages

<table>
<tr><td>Page numbering starting at 1</td><td>

1 Tap <u>Esc</u> for Escape
2 Tap <u>F</u> for Format
3 Tap <u>D</u> for Division
4 Tap <u>P</u> for Page-numbers
5 Tap the <u>Spacebar</u> to select **FORMAT DIVISION PAGE-NUMBERS: (Yes)**
6 Tap <u>Enter</u>. Printed pages will now be numbered, starting with 1, until **FORMAT DIVISION PAGE-NUMBERS: (No)** is selected again

</td></tr>
<tr><td>Page numbering not starting at 1</td><td>

1 Follow steps 1–5 above to switch on page numbering. (**Do not tap** <u>Enter</u>)
2 Tap the <u>↓</u>, <u>Down</u>, key once to arrive at **numbering: (Continuous)**
3 Tap the <u>Spacebar</u> once to select **numbering: (Start)**
4 Tap the <u>→</u>, <u>Right</u>, key once. In response to the prompt **at:**
5 TYPE the number of the page with which page numbering is to start; eg 12
6 Tap <u>Enter</u>. Page numbers will now start at 12 when the document is printed

The page number is shown in the Status Line. It is printed 0.5" from the top and 7.25" from the left side of a page. If the right margin is altered move the page number to keep the two in alignment, if so desired.

</td></tr>
</table>

Memory jogger	To cancel a command, tap <u>Esc</u> for Escape. The active cursor will again be in the window.
Text creation	1 TYPE <u>Your Own Name</u> 2 Tap <u>Enter</u> 3 times 3 TYPE in the text of Task 33
Amendments	1 Proofread your work and correct any mistakes you find 2 Move the cursor to the first letter of the third paragraph (the 'T' of 'The page...') 3 Hold down <u>Ctrl</u> and <u>Shift</u> together and tap Enter to force a page break 4 Switch on page numbering starting at 1 5 PRINT the two pages 6 Renumber the pages 12 and 13 7 PRINT them again

SAVE your work (filename: <u>YourInitials33</u>, *see* Task 4). Record its details in your manual log (Task 6).

Task 33

DESKTOP PUBLISHING

The need for expensive typesetting machinery or in-house printing
departments has been greatly reduced by the advent of desktop
publishing systems.

A typical desktop publishing system consists of a personal computer
connected to a laser printer, using powerful word processing and page
layout software.

The page layout software and the laser printer make the big difference
compared with traditional methods. Pages can be typeset onscreen and
different versions tried out without the need for referral back to
typesetters.

The laser printer can be linked to a large number of terminals working
independently, which maximises its usefulness.

Appendix

Setting the line counter: (*see* The screen on page 2)

Tap ⃞Esc⃞ape, ⃞O⃞ptions. Tap ⃞↑⃞, ⃞UP⃞, 3 times.
In response to the prompt: **Line numbers: Yes(No)** tap the ⃞Spacebar⃞ once to select (**Yes**).
Tap ⃞Enter⃞. Lines will be counted until (**No**) is selected.

Toggle keys (*see* page 5)

The keystrokes taught on page 5 are not the only toggle keys in Word. The full set is shown in the diagram below in the positions in which they appear in the Status Line. The circled two-letter codes are taught in this *Guide*. If both of any of the five pairs of locking keys are switched on, the only code that appears onscreen is the code in the upper row.

		1	2	3	4	5	6	
Status Line:	**Pg1 Li19 Co30** {}	**LY**	(**LD**)	**ZM**	(**CS**)	(**OT**)	**RM**	**Microsoft Word**
Hidden codes (see above)		(**CL**)	(**NL**)	(**SL**)	(**EX**)		**ST**	

Cancelling toggle keys

To cancel the toggle keys (without circles) shown above:

LY	⃞Alt+F4⃞
ZM	⃞Ctrl+F1⃞
ST	⃞Ctrl+F3⃞
RM	⃞Shift+F3⃞

Toggle case To change the case of words highlighted by the cursor, hold down Ctrl and tap F4 (ie Ctrl+F4). The highlighted text is taken one step through the sequence: upper case, initial capitals, lower case, upper case, initial capitals etc. For example, if you highlighted 'word processing' and tapped Ctrl+F4 repeatedly, then it would become:

WORD PROCESSING — first
Word Processing — second
word processing — third and so on

See page 5 for switching the other toggle keys.

Short cuts Some commands may be speeded up using the following keystrokes:

Save Ctrl+F10   Saves the document onscreen if it has already been given a filename. If the document has no filename, you will be taken to the **TRANSFER SAVE filename:** prompt. See Task 4

Print Ctrl+F8   Prints the document onscreen. See Task 8

Load Ctrl+F7   Takes you to the **TRANSFER LOAD filename:** prompt and displays files with the '.DOC' filename extension in the directory. See Tasks 5 and 6

Tabs Alt+F1   Takes you to the FORMAT TABS set: prompt. See Task 21.